Air-to-Air Refuelling Aircraft

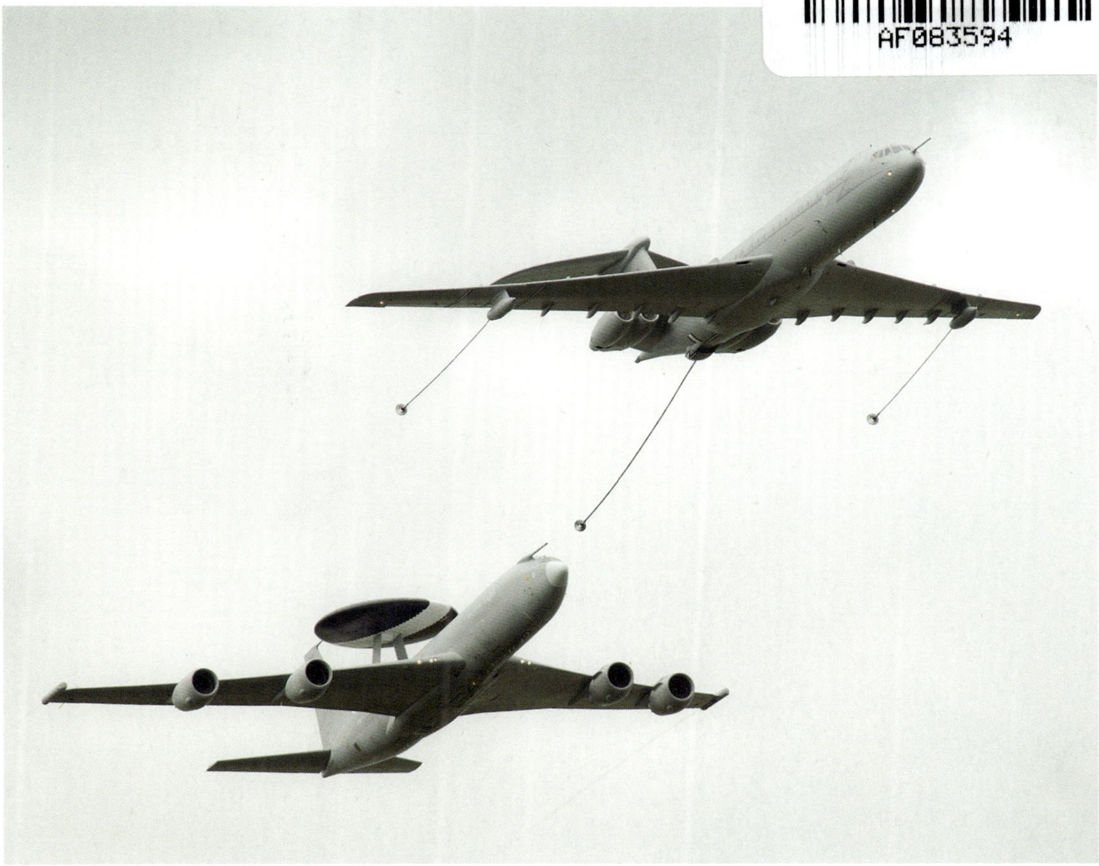

CHRIS GIBSON

KEY Books

MODERN MILITARY AIRCRAFT SERIES, VOLUME 3

Front cover image: Photographed from a Hercules' astrodome during a refuelling operation, the VC10 tanker has flaps and leading-edge slats deployed to match the speed of the Hercules receiver. (MOD/Open Government Licence)

Back cover image: High over the North Sea, 101 Sqn Vickers VC10 K3 ZA148 refuels English Electric Lightning F6 XR771 of XI Sqn. Lightnings were regular users of the RAF's tanker force on air defence sorties and deployments. (Blue Envoy Collection)

Title page image: The Royal Air Force has, since the 1970s, appreciated the value of force multipliers in the form of an air refuelling fleet of tankers and an airborne early warning squadron. The Vickers VC10 and the Boeing E-3D Sentry enabled the RAF to punch well above its weight on operations. (© Graham Wheatley, 2010)

Contents page image: Old meets new over the Mojave Desert. Northrop YF-17s (72-1569 and 72-1570) undergo refuelling trials with an Air National Guard Boeing KC-97L during the USAF's Lightweight Fighter fly-off in 1974. (Terry Panopalis Collection)

Published by Key Books
An imprint of Key Publishing Ltd
PO Box 100
Stamford
Lincs PE19 1XQ

www.keypublishing.com

The right of Chris Gibson to be identified as the author of this book has been asserted in accordance with the Copyright, Designs and Patents Act 1988 Sections 77 and 78.

Copyright © Chris Gibson, 2021

ISBN 978 1 913870 69 0

All rights reserved. Reproduction in whole or in part in any form whatsoever or by any means is strictly prohibited without the prior permission of the Publisher.

Typeset by SJmagic DESIGN SERVICES, India.

Contents

Introduction		4
Chapter 1	Tankers – The Essential Force Multiplier	7
Chapter 2	Pioneers	9
Chapter 3	The Big Stick – SAC and TAC	12
Chapter 4	The Tanker War – Vietnam and Tactical Support	24
Chapter 5	Reach – USAF Strategic Logistics	30
Chapter 6	Deterrence to Air Defence – RAF Tankers	37
Chapter 7	Private Practice	57
Chapter 8	Rotary Refuelling – Helicopters	63
Chapter 9	Trials and Tankers	68
Chapter 10	Buddies	71
Chapter 11	Dozapravka vs Polete	82
Chapter 12	Les Revitailleurs – Sous-Marine	88
Chapter 13	The 707 Tankers	90
Conclusion		94
Select Bibliography		95
Glossary		96

Introduction

Force multipliers – techniques or equipment that enable a military service to conduct operations that would not be possible without them.

An example of a force multiplier is the machine gun, which gave one soldier the firepower of an entire battalion. In air warfare, perhaps the finest examples of force multipliers as key to victory were the Chain Home radar and Filter Rooms of the Battle of Britain. These enabled Fighter Command to place its limited fighter resources in the right place at the right time rather than conduct resource-sapping continuous patrols.

Any modern air force that hopes to be taken seriously on the world stage needs to possess, or have access to, force multipliers, and one of the most important is in-flight refuelling. This became practical

Tanker, boom, boom/drogue adapter and probe seen from the cockpit of a Grumman A-6 Intruder (or possibly an EA-6 Prowler). This photo sums up the world of in-flight refuelling by showing a US Navy aircraft fitted for probe-and-drogue refuelling, taking fuel from a USAF KC-135 through a flying boom fitted with a Boom/Drogue Adapter. (Via Robert S Hopkins III)

in the mid-1940s but for almost half a century remained the forte of the largest of air forces, only becoming more widely used from the early 1990s, in the post-Cold War era.

The importance of this capability can be summed up in a single campaign. Possession of strategic and tactical air-to-air refuelling capabilities made the air support of the war in Afghanistan possible. In-flight refuelling enabled strategic bombers such as Rockwell B-1Bs, Grumman B-2s and Boeing B-52s to fly what were effectively close support missions, sometimes direct from bases in in the continental United States. Tankers also enabled US naval aircraft from carriers in the Arabian Sea and RAF aircraft from bases in the Gulf states to provide persistent support over Afghanistan. This campaign also applied the lessons of inter-service co-operation on refuelling learned in the 1991 Gulf War.

It was an earlier war that cemented the tanker's place in air forces' order of battle. The Falklands Conflict of 1982 demonstrated how tankers could not only support fighters and bombers but also other

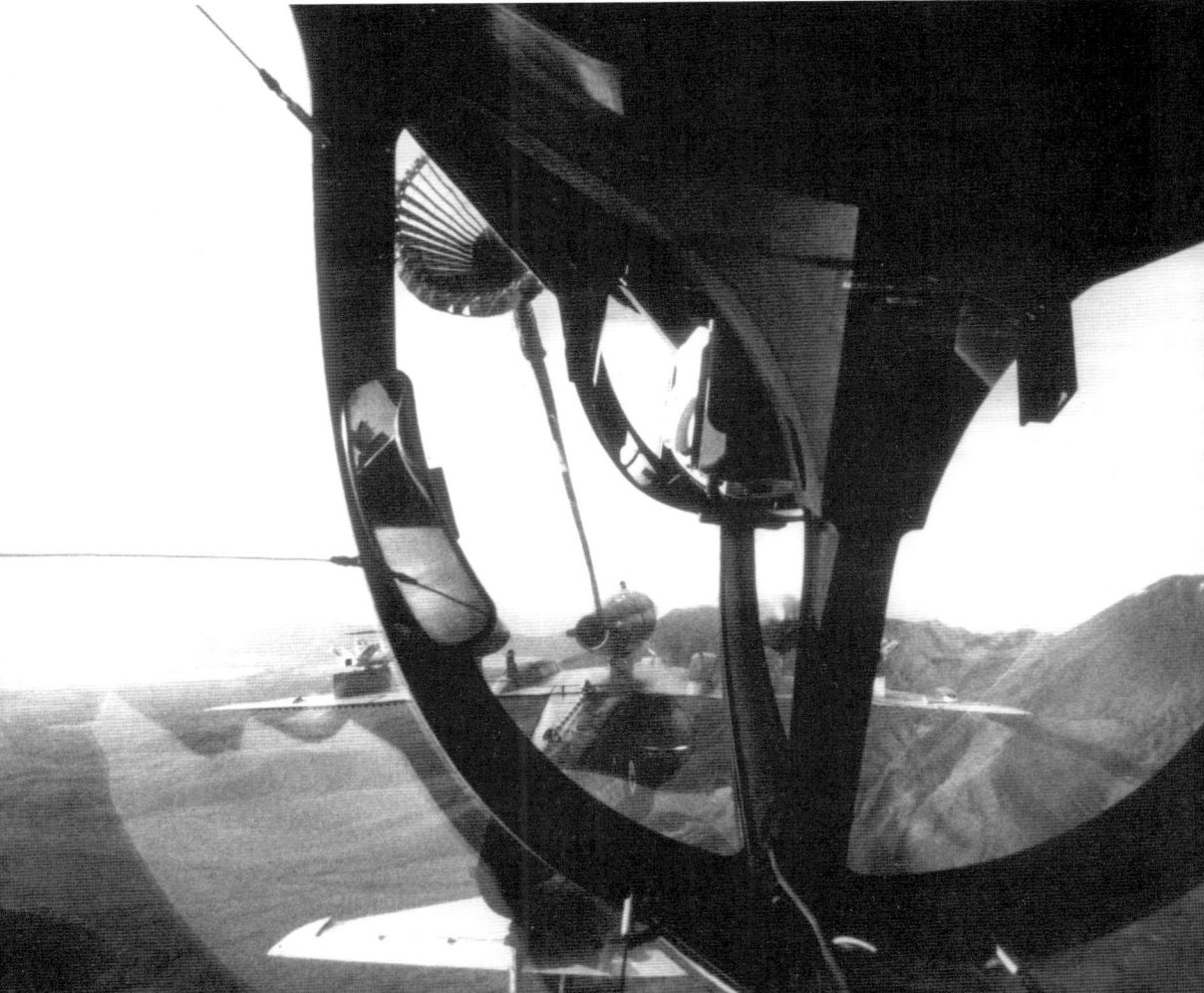

Mention of in-flight refuelling conjures up the image of a converted airliner or bomber making sedate progress through the air with a gaggle of fighters in tow. Not so for the RNZAF! Who else could fly inverted, in contact, over an active volcano? Two RNZAF TA-4K Skyhawks in refuelling contact fly over Mt Ruapehu. Inverted (RNZAF)

The Handley Page Victor K2 was key to the RAF's operations in the South Atlantic, and without Victor support the *Black Buck* missions and Hercules logistics operations could not have happened. As a result, the RAF's tanker force was expanded and improved. (Blue Envoy Collection)

support aircraft such as transports and maritime patrol types. Having supported the longest bombing missions to date and putting an anti-submarine and search-and-rescue capability over a war zone 3,400nm (6,300km) away, tankers became the essential force multiplier. The lessons of the Falklands Conflict did not go unnoticed, especially in the UK, with an expansion of tanker fleets and the rise of the tanker/transport. From being in the order of battle of the major powers such as France, UK, USA and USSR in 1980, by the turn of the century, tanker aircraft were parked on the ramps of air forces around the world. Long derided as mere support acts for the fighters and bombers, the truth is that a modern air force equipped with the latest generation of multi-role combat aircraft cannot operate to its optimum capacity without these force multipliers.

Chapter 1

Tankers – The Essential Force Multiplier

'The only time an aircraft has too much fuel on board is when it is on fire.'
Attributed to either Charles Kingsford-Smith or Ernest K Gann
'Nobody kicks ass without tanker gas.' Anyone who has been KC-135 crew.

The view from the boom operator's station on a Boeing KC-135 tanker over South East Asia in May 1970. A pair of McDonnell Douglas F-4C Phantom IIs from 433TFS, 8TFW loaded with bombs take on 'tanker gas' before 'kicking ass'. Tankers of all the US services made the intense air operations of the Vietnam War possible. (Terry Panopalis Collection)

The Case for Tankers

Endurance, range and radius of action are all expressions of the time and/or distance over which an aircraft can deliver its payload, be that weapons, cargo or passengers. All three depend on the amount of fuel available to the aircraft's engines, no matter how efficient those engines may be. For the first half century of powered flight, operational aircraft could only burn fuel they could carry internally or externally in 'drop tanks'. These first appeared during the Spanish Civil War but became a common sight on combat aircraft from 1940, and when used by Allied escort fighters, drop tanks had, according to Prof R V Jones, 'changed the balance of air warfare against Germany in 1944.' Drop tanks enabled more fuel to be carried, and when the fuel was used up, as the name suggests, they could be dropped. The benefit was mainly in being able to carry more fuel without enlarging the airframe, which would have weight and drag penalties. Unfortunately, the aircraft had to burn more fuel lifting the extra fuel off the ground and overcome the aerodynamic drag of the tank. Despite these technical characteristics, the drop tank was a war winner, at least in Europe.

The Pacific War was different. Consider the Pacific Ocean, its vastness covering almost a hemisphere, and the distance from San Francisco to Tokyo, 4,460nm (8,260km), is twice the distance from San Francisco to New York, 2,235nm (4,139km). As noted above, fighters and even long-range bombers were limited by the fuel they could carry. From 1942, the USAAF examined using the Consolidated B-24 as a tanker to refuel Boeing B-17s in flight, with trials underway when the air-to-air refuelling programme was shelved. The reason for the cancellation was the commitment in 1942 to the Hemisphere Defense Weapon that was intended to carry a ton of bombs for 4,634nm (8,582km), leading to the development of the long-range Boeing B-29 and Consolidated B-32.

Even with the long range provided by the B-29 and B-32, to take the bomber offensive to the Japanese home islands required a costly amphibious campaign by the US Navy, Marine Corps and Army to capture islands where aircraft could be based for an aerial campaign against Japan. After brutal fighting and heavy casualties, October 1944 saw Japan within the range of land-based bombers from the Marianas and from March 1945, land-based single-engine fighters from Iwo Jima.

With the end of the war in Europe in May 1945, the RAF considered using inflight refuelling for the Lancasters and, later, Lincolns committed to Tiger Force in the Far East. The RAF operated mainly in the Burma theatre in support of General Slim's 14th Army, but after the defeat of Germany, Britain's attention turned to Japan. Set up in mid-1945, Tiger Force was to conduct a bombing offensive against Japan in preparation for Operation *Downfall*, the invasion of Japan planned for 1946. Tiger Force was to set Bomber Command's Avro Lancasters and new Lincoln Mk.1s to work in the destruction of the Japanese war economy. However, designed for use against Germany, they lacked the range for a war on the scale of the Pacific theatre. Avro addressed this in late 1944 by installing a saddle tank behind the cockpit, with two Lancasters receiving this modification, but the 1,200 imp gal (5,455ltr) of fuel, over 9,300lb (4,250kg), in the tank affected handling at high weights and was soon cancelled. By July 1945, US forces had captured Okinawa, which meant that a fuel tank installed in the bomb bay was deemed sufficient for Lancaster operations from Okinawa. Japan surrendered on 15th August, six days after the USAAF dropped a second atomic bomb, and the cessation of hostilities saw all plans for the Tiger Force cancelled.

The drop tank made a major contribution to the air war in Western Europe, and in an attempt to extend the range of the Spitfire Mk.IX as an escort fighter, two Mk.IXs were fitted with drop tanks from a Mustang. The trouble with drop tanks is that the extra weight has to be lifted and contributes drag until they are dropped. (Blue Envoy Collection)

Chapter 2

Pioneers

The earliest tests of refuelling aircraft in flight were undertaken in the USA in the early 1920s. These involved lowering cans of fuel on a rope between the aircraft. Transfer by hose would allow useful volumes of fuel to be moved from the tanker to the receiver and make the practice worthwhile. One of the earliest examples of the practice occurred on 27 June 1923 during an endurance attempt by the US Army Air Service with two de Havilland DH.4bs. The tanker DH.4b trailed a hose that was captured by the rear crewman in the receiver who attached it to the receiver's fuel tanks. Once connected, fuel was transferred by gravity feed. (Blue Envoy Collection)

In addition to the saddle tank, the Air Staff had looked at another method of increasing the range of its Lancasters and Lincolns for the Pacific War: refuelling in flight. The Americans had pioneered the procedure in June 1923, when the first air-to-air refuelling took place between two Airco DH.4Bs. The initial work involved those daredevils of 1920s air displays, wing walkers, who strapped cans of petrol to their backs and moved between aircraft. While making for a thrilling spectacle at an airshow, this was hardly a practical proposition for a bomber of transport.

Practical Air-to-Air Refuelling

A vast improvement on wing walkers moving between aircraft carrying cans of petrol on their backs, the first recorded use of a hose to transfer fuel between aircraft occurred on 27 June 1923 during an attempt on an endurance record. A US Army Air Service de Havilland DH.4b 'tanker' passed a hose to another DH.4b, becoming the first 'receiver' with the hose manhandled from the rear cockpit of the 'tanker' and passed to the 'receiver' flying below. Once the observer in the receiver had placed the nozzle into the fuel tank filler and opened the valve, the fuel was gravity fed from the tanker. A century on, transfer of fuel by hose is the most common in-flight refuelling method in use.

With an empire to connect, the British opted to transport passengers and especially mail by air. Although much of the Empire could be reached by overland routes with refuelling stops, the transatlantic route was a different matter. Although not first to perform it, the pioneer of in-flight refuelling in the UK was Alan Cobham, who from 1932 investigated a practical method for transferring fuel from one aircraft, the tanker, to a second, the receiver.

Cobham's aim was to increase the range of the airliners that connected the far-flung outposts of the British Empire and reduce the need for time-consuming refuelling stops en route to Australia and South Africa. A further goal was to enable transatlantic air travel that was faster than the airships in service at the time. In 1934, Cobham set up a company, Flight Refuelling Ltd (FRL), to develop what Cobham called the 'looped-hose method' for commercial aviation, and in the years leading up to the Second World War, FRL investigated in-flight refuelling for Imperial Airways. The airline planned to use in-flight refuelling for its transatlantic flying boat services, and FRL was by 1939 conducting trials of Cobham's looped-hose system. The equipment was fitted to an FRL-operated Handley Page Harrow, G-AFRL, that was used as a tanker to refuel Imperial Airways' Short S.23 Empire Class flying boats such as G-AFCU *Cabot*.

The FRL technique involved some complex and intricate manoeuvres by the aircraft and specialist equipment such as a grapple, a line and a hose, with the receiver's crew using a line and grapple to

Transatlantic routes posed a problem for the pre-war airlines. Imperial Airways planned to use Empire Class flying boats, but these lacked the range of their American counterparts and a solution was sought. Alan Cobham pioneered air-to-air refuelling in the UK and set up Flight Refuelling Ltd (FRL) in 1934. In the years leading up to the Second World War, Imperial Airways was planning on using in-flight refuelling on its transatlantic services. FRL was, by 1939, conducting trials of Alan Cobham's looped-hose system on Imperial Airways' Short S.23 flying boats such as G-AFCU, with FRL operating Handley Page Harrow G-AFRL as the tanker. (Blue Envoy Collection)

capture the tanker's hose, haul the hose into the cabin, connect it to the receiver's fuel system and commence transfer. Despite requiring a lot of manpower, by 1939, Alan Cobham's techniques were being used on Handley Page Harrow transports and had by the outbreak of war, refuelled Short Empire C-Class flying boats on 15 transatlantic flights. But for the outbreak of the Second World War, these trials would have continued and led to a more practical system.

Development stopped for the duration, but as noted above, in 1945 the Air Staff examined this using FRL's equipment to extend the endurance of the Tiger Force. The end of the war saw renewed American interest in the looped-hose technique, and it was modified for use on pressurised aircraft such as the Boeing B-29 Superfortress. FRL recognised the looped-hose method's limitations and by 1949 had developed what became the now-familiar 'probe-and-drogue' system, which the British adopted after trials had shown it to be a capable and practical system. Aside from controlling a winch and switching on pumps, which could be done by the flight engineer, the process more or less required no manpower.

FRL continued work on the probe-and-drogue system, and an FRL Mk.VII hose drum (HDU) unit was installed in the Avro Lancaster G-33-2, and as development continued, in the Avro Lincoln RA657 with both tankers conducting refuelling trials using Gloster Meteor F2s fitted with probes in the nose. By early 1949, the USAF, which had been following FRL's work, requested that a Boeing B-29 Superfortress be converted into a single-point tanker with a Mk.VII HDU, with another B-29 modified as a three-point tanker. Two USAF Republic F-84 Thunderjets and a pair of B-29s were converted to receivers. Trials went well, with the two B-29 tankers refuelling the B-29 and F-84 receivers, proving the probe-and-drogue system's superiority over the looped-hose method. The US Air Force subsequently replaced all its looped-hose kit with probe-and-drogue equipment on its aircraft.

Since the method worked well for small aircraft that were agile enough to perform the fine manoeuvres required to make contact with the drogue, the US Navy also adopted it for its carrier aircraft. Compact and light, the hose and drogue system could be packaged as an HDU that fitted in a modified drop tank, producing the 'buddy pack' to convert any aircraft into a tanker. The first buddy-buddy refuelling was carried out by two North American F-100D Super Sabres in December 1956.

After the war, Cobham and his company, FRL, returned to developing refuelling systems, and with the looped-hose proving complex, the hose and drogue took over. The system was fitted to Avro Lancaster G-33-2, which was used for refuelling trials with Gloster Meteors fitted with probes. (Wiki Commons)

Chapter 3
The Big Stick – SAC and TAC

As relations between the wartime Allies cooled, and the USSR became viewed as a threat to the Western democracies, the USAAF planned for intercontinental bomber operations against the Soviet Union, and, to this end, Strategic Air Command (SAC) was established in March 1946. The power projection made available by the Boeing B-29/B-50 'Hemisphere Defense Weapon' was soon enhanced by the Convair B-36, Boeing B-47 and B-52. The B-36 was developed to bomb Germany from Newfoundland and later, Japan from Hawaii, but arrived too late for the Second World War. The B-47 and B-52 were designed to deliver atomic weapons on targets in the Soviet Union, a vast expanse that stretched 3,500nm (6,482km) from Smolensk in the west to Naukan in the east – analogous to the Pacific Ocean of the previous war. In addition, the aircraft had to first reach the Soviet border from bases in the USA or Western Europe before flying deep into Soviet territory.

During a mission to circumnavigate the Earth, Boeing B-50A 46-0010 *Lucky Lady II* was refuelled by a Boeing KB-29 using the looped-hose method. From take-off on 26 February 1949, the flight lasted 94 hours, and *Lucky Lady II* was refuelled four times by KB-29s of the 43rd Air Refuelling Squadron. The refuelling took place over the Azores, Saudi Arabia, the Philippines and Hawaii. The main differences between the B-29 and the B-50A can be seen in this image with the taller tailfin and modified nacelles for the Pratt & Whitney R-4360 engines most obvious. (Blue Envoy Collection)

To meet the challenge of bombing Germany from the USA, or Japan from Hawaii, the Consolidated B-36 had to be large enough to carry the fuel to cross the oceans. Post-war, the sheer size of the Soviet Union, on top of the distance to its borders, made in-flight refuelling a must-have capability. (Blue Envoy Collection)

The turbojet-powered Boeing B-47 and B-52 were thirsty beasts, and to reach their targets, in-flight refuelling was required. Two elements soon became obvious: the probe-and-drogue system, with its flexible hoses could not support the flow rates required to rapidly refuel a large bomber. The other was that a fatigued bomber crew returning from a long mission might not be capable of performing the aerial ballet required to place the probe in the drogue.

The probe-and-drogue system could lead to multiple abortive attempts at contact before a successful transfer, and this could result in broken probes (usually the valve on the end of the probe). The fuel flow rates, typically 360–700 US gal/min (1,360–2,700l/min), while sufficient for fighters and strike aircraft, were unsuitable for large aircraft such as heavy bombers, which required higher transfer rates. This led to Boeing developing the flying boom system that comprised a telescopic tube fitted with a pair of control surfaces that an operator in the tanker used to guide the boom nozzle into a receptacle on the receiving aircraft. The receiver flew in close formation aft of the tanker, and once within the boom's operating envelope, the boom operator 'flew' the nozzle into the receptacle. The larger diameter plumbing on the boom enabled much higher flow rates, typically 900–1,020 US gal/min (3,410–3,864l/min), providing quicker, larger volume top-ups that were particularly suited to bombers.

The flying boom was developed by Boeing and has been fitted to Boeing's KB-29, KC-97, KC-135 and KC-46A aircraft, as well as variants of the basic concept on the McDonnell Douglas KC-10 Extender, such as the McDonnell Douglas advanced aerial refuelling boom (AARB) and the Airbus Industrie A330 MRTT. The latter is fitted with a variation on the flying boom called the Advanced Aerial

Refuelling Boom System (AARBS) developed by Airbus Military, which is compatible with USAF receptacles. Another innovation from Airbus is the SMART refuelling system that allows automatic boom deployment once the receiver aircraft is in position.

One notable, and record-setting, event in the early days of in-flight refuelling was a mission to circumnavigate the Earth non-stop, during which Boeing B-50A 46-0010 *Lucky Lady II* was refuelled by Boeing KB-29s using the looped-hose method. From take-off on 26 February 1949, the flight lasted 94 hours and *Lucky Lady II* was refuelled four times by KB-29s of the 43rd Air Refuelling Squadron, with the refuelling operations taking place over the Azores, Saudi Arabia, the Philippines and Hawaii. The operation showed that the USA not only had a monopoly on atomic weapons but had the means to deliver ordnance anywhere, anytime.

In addition to supporting SAC's heavy bombers, the Boeing KB-29 fleet refuelled SAC's extensive fleet of fighters such as Republic F-84G Thunderjets. These, the successors to the escort fighters of the Second World War and separate from Tactical Air Command (TAC) and its fighters, would need to deploy to Europe in the event of war. Operation *Longstride* in 1950 was the first major deployment to use in-flight refuelling, as previous operations had been 'island-hopping' affairs with stops in the Azores or Iceland. As the Cold War continued, and with the availability of smaller tactical nuclear weapons, fighters such as the nuclear capable Republic F-84G performed tanker-supported transatlantic deployments to Europe in support of the 'Trip Wire' response. The F-84G was the first US fighter to carry nuclear weapons and be capable of flying boom refuelling, with *Longstride* demonstrating these could be deployed to Europe at short notice.

The Trip Wire strategy adopted by the Western Powers required massive retaliation with nuclear weapons against Soviet targets. As the size of nuclear weapons reduced, these could be carried by Strategic Air Command's fleet of fighters including the Republic F-84G Thunderjet. The first USAF single-engine fighter capable of carrying a nuclear weapon, the F-84G could be refuelled by the same flying boom technique as SAC's heavy bombers. Without air-to-air refuelling, moving these fighters from the USA to Europe would have been lengthy affairs with fuel stops in Iceland or the Azores so in 1950, SAC conducted Operation *Longstride*. This, the first of many such operations, involved Boeing KB-29 tankers and showed that non-stop transatlantic deployments of single-engined fighter-bombers were possible if supported by enough tankers. (Blue Envoy Collection)

One reason that the USAF looked unfavourably upon the probe-and-drogue system was that the drogue was unstable. Boeing KB-29 tankers initially used a solid 'funnel' to guide the receiver's probe into the connector. The solid drogue moved around too much in the tanker's slipstream and was soon replaced with more stable, slotted drogues or a basket composed of spokes that enabled air to flow through them. This latter type also had an additional benefit of being collapsible, which enabled them to be more easily stowed in a pod or HDU fairing when the hose was hauled in. The boom/drogue adapter (BDA) for the Boeing KC-135 still uses a slotted metal drogue.

Having been replaced in the early 1950s by the jet-powered Boeing B-47 Stratojet, much of the B-50 fleet was converted by Haynes Industries to replace TAC's KB-29 fleet, with 136 B-50s fitted with a three-point hose-and-drogue system and large underwing tanks. The later KB-50J featured two General Electric J47 auxiliary turbojets to reduce the speed differential as more advanced types such as the Century Series entered TAC service. The KB-50 fleet supported USAF tactical aircraft such as the Douglas B-66 Destroyer, a type that, while designed as a bomber, would gain fame in the Vietnam War as a photoreconnaissance, electronic intelligence (ELINT), electronic warfare and trials aircraft.

A receiver's eye view of an early drogue trailed by a Boeing KB-29 tanker. The solid drogue seen here tended to move around in the tanker's turbulent slipstream. These 'funnels' were replaced with a collapsible wire basket or a slotted design. (Blue Envoy Collection)

The F-100 Super Sabre (aka The Hun) was a TAC stalwart, and this Super Sabre 58-1217 from the 8TFW Pacific Air Forces is taking fuel from the wing tip pod of a KB-50J. The configuration of the KB-50J's refuelling equipment and turbojets is visible, and of note are the Hun's deployed leading-edge slats and nose-up attitude. (Terry Panopalis Collection)

Left: One of the tasks for TAC's KB-50 tankers was deployment of tactical aircraft from the USA to Europe. These KB-50Js (note the turbojet under the outer wings) from 4505th Air Refuelling Wing based at Langley AFB are refuelling Douglas B-66 Destroyers being deployed to Europe in September 1961. (NARA via Terry Panopalis)

Below: The speed differential between the Boeing B-52 and the KC-97 is illustrated by this image of a B-52B on the boom of a KC-97 in the early days of B-52 development during the mid-1950s. The B-52 has its undercarriage lowered and has adopted a nose-up attitude to maintain station behind the KC-97. (Blue Envoy Collection)

The Big Stick – SAC and TAC

The USAF's first 'strategic' tanker was the Boeing KC-97, the refuelling variant of the C-97 Stratofreighter transport aircraft. The KC-97 initially provided refuelling support for SAC's Boeing B-50 Superfortress fleet but proved more important in refuelling Boeing B-47 Stratojets. The B-50 and KC-97 were evenly matched performance-wise, but as the jet-powered B-47 and B-52 entered service, the speed differential made the KC-97 effectively obsolete in SAC.

In support of the Boeing B-47 fleet, especially the RB-47s on reconnaissance flights, the KC-97 required two separate fuel systems: Avgas for its Pratt & Whitney R-4360-59 Wasp Major piston engines and kerosene for the receiver's turbojets. The KC-97 also lacked the speed and altitude performance of the new generation of jets. The speed differential between the Boeing B-52 and the KC-97 was such that the B-52 had to lower its undercarriage and adopt a nose-up attitude to maintain station behind the KC-97. The initial solution was to refuel in a shallow dive, but ultimately the KC-97s were fitted with the J47 turbojets from the KB-50Js to become KC-97Ls. Interestingly, in the 1980s the RAF had the opposite problem with fast tankers (Victors) and slow receivers (Hercules) – the solution being the same: refuel in a shallow dive!

The KC-97 soldiered on until 1978, flying with TAC, Air Force Reserve and various Air National Guards while the Spanish Air Force operated a trio of KC-97Ls in the 1970s and acquired another two for spares.

The transition from piston to turbine saw SAC's Boeing B-50 and Convair B-36 fleets superseded by Boeing's B-47 Stratojet. These jet bombers were thirsty, powered by six General Electric J47 turbojets and would have required a great deal of tanker support to carry out their strategic bombing role. Once the receiver was on the boom, the KC-97 could transfer fuel at a rate of 600 US gal/min (2,271l/min), but this was deemed too low for operations with the B-52 and resulted in the KC-97's replacement being fitted with transfer pumps capable of up to 1,000 US gal/min (3,785l/min). The rate could be varied depending on the receiver, with the limit on the transfer rate being the plumbing of the receiver's fuel system.

Strategic Air Command's primary tanker in the mid-1950s was the piston-engined Boeing KC-97, and this view from a KC-97's boom operator's station shows an early Boeing B-47 with the refuelling receptacle offset to starboard in the extreme nose. The KC-97 soon proved too slow and lacked the fuel transfer rates required by SAC's new generation of jet-powered strategic bombers. (Blue Envoy Collection)

Later versions of the Boeing B-47, particularly the reconnaissance variants with revised sensor packages in the nose, such as the RB-47H, had their receptacle moved to a position on the centreline just forward of the windscreen. This RB-47H is being refuelled from a KC-135, the words 'HIGH SPEED BOOM' visible on the control planes. (Terry Panopalis Collection)

Keeping the Pentagon's 'Big Stick' in the air required a tanker that was faster, higher flying and delivered more fuel faster. Addressing the need for a tanker with higher performance to support the new generation of bombers such as the Boeing B-52 Stratofortress and Convair B-58 Hustler, Boeing developed the KC-135 Stratotanker. 'More than just a tanker', the KC-135 formed the basis of a multitude of support types for the USAF in more than 60 years of service and is destined to remain operational for the foreseeable future.

More Than a Tanker

By 1959, the USAF had a high-speed transport and dedicated tanker in the form of the fast, high-flying Boeing C-135 Stratolifter and the more numerous KC-135 Stratotanker, both derived from the Boeing Model 360-80 jet transport demonstrator. The 'Dash 80' also led to the Boeing 707 airliner that has also formed the basis of tanker aircraft converted from surplus airline stock.

One reason SAC needed its dedicated fleet of tankers was the maintenance of a deterrent that could immediately react to any sign of Soviet aggression, and from 1960 until 1968, SAC maintained a constant airborne deterrent with Operation *Chrome Dome*. Bombers such as the Boeing B-52, armed with nuclear weapons, and supported by KC-135 Stratotankers, followed routes from their bases in the United States to take them close to Soviet airspace. Three main routes were followed: east over the Atlantic and into the Mediterranean, northwest to Alaska and northeast to Baffin Island and Greenland.

One type that required a faster, higher-flying tanker like the KC-135 was the Convair B-58 Hustler, SAC's high-speed penetrator. Designed for high-altitude/high-speed penetration of Soviet airspace, the change in the mid-1960s to low-level operations meant that its afterburning General Electric J79s were operating well below their optimum altitude, and this increased its fuel consumption, placing further

As SAC fielded the faster and higher-flying B-52 and B-58, a tanker with higher performance than the KC-97J was required. The resulting KC-135 entered service in 1957 and still serves alongside the B-52. This example is refuelling a Convair B-58 Hustler during a 1963 test flight by the Air Force Flight Test Center and is carrying the combined fuel/weapons pod on the centreline, plus four Mk.43 nuclear weapons on the ventral pylons. (AFFTC via Terry Panopalis)

Keeping the Pentagon's 'Big Stick' in the air was the main task of the tanker fleet in the early 1960s, exemplified by this B-52D Stratofortress on the boom of a KC-135 Stratotanker. 'More than just a tanker' the KC-135 formed the basis of a multitude of support types for the USAF over more than 60 years in service and is destined to remain in service for the foreseeable future. (Blue Envoy Collection)

reliance on the tanker fleet, especially since B-58s were rarely forward-based in Europe. This change of mission profile was one of the many factors that led to the Hustler's retirement after ten years in service.

The KC-135A Stratotanker used the same Pratt & Whitney J57 engines as the B-52, and thus possessed the performance to match the new generation of bombers. The water injection system increased available thrust by 30% and made for spectacularly noisy and smoky take-offs. As engine technology advanced, 157 KC-135s were converted to turbofan power by fitting Pratt & Whitney TF33 engines from retired Boeing 707 airliners to produce the KC-135E. The TF33s produced 80% more thrust than the J57s of the KC-135A but were 14% more fuel efficient, which in turn enabled a 20% increase in fuel offload. The remaining KC-135As were fitted with CFM56 high bypass ratio turbofans that provide double the thrust of the original J57 with a 25% increase in fuel efficiency to produce the KC-135R. The CFM56 engines enabled up to 60% more range and a fuel offload that was 50% greater than the A-model. One more obvious benefit of the engine update was the cleaner exhaust and much reduced noise level. The engine upgrades along with new systems have enabled the KC-135 to remain in service for 60 years, raising the possibility of a century of service with the USAF.

The KC-135 is 'More Than a Tanker' and has formed the basis of a vast range of specialist types including special reconnaissance, command post, transport and trials aircraft. The RAF's three AirSeeker R1 electronic reconnaissance aircraft of 51 Squadron were converted to RC-135W Rivet Joint standard from former USAF KC-135R aircraft.

Aside from the plethora of specialist reconnaissance and command post variants, the KC-135 is most famous for the Q variant that was used to support development flying of the Lockheed YF-12A interceptor and operational use of the A-12 and SR-71 Blackbird reconnaissance types. Owing to these reconnaissance aircrafts' use of specialised fuel (low volatility JP-7), the KC-135Q required two separate fuel systems and carried JP-7 fuel in tanks in the main cabin, filled via a pair of connectors in one of the main undercarriage bays. Delivery to the A-12, YF-12 and SR-71 required a specially modified boom that enabled refuelling

Alaskan air power includes Alaskan Air National Guard KC-135E tankers and General Dynamics F-16s, based at Eielson AFB near Fairbanks. Standard procedure is for the receiver to form up in echelon aft of the tanker on the port side, move in to refuel and, on completion, move to the starboard side of the tanker. (Via Robert S Hopkins III)

The KC-135 proved highly suitable for conversion to other roles such as electronic intelligence gathering (ELINT) which saw a variety of antennas added to the basic airframe. This RC-135U with Combat Sent modifications is 'on the boom' of a KC-135. The RC-135U series was fitted with the TF33 turbofan. (Jeffrey Harper via Robert S Hopkins III)

While the KC-135 has been exported to four foreign countries, only one has procured the RC-135V Rivet Joint. The RAF operates three AirSeeker R1s that replaced the Nimrod R1P. The AirSeekers retain the USAF boom receptacle and, unlike the Boeing E-3D Sentries, have not been fitted with a probe to allow refuelling from the RAF's own tanker fleet. (MOD/Open Government Licence)

at the KC-135Q's maximum air speed. The boom also included a hard wire communications system to enable radio silence to be maintained during contacts. The KC-135Q was critical to the operation of the SR-71 as the machine took off with a light fuel load and had to 'warm up' its airframe to energise the seals on the fuel system. The aircraft required fuelling before and after a high-speed intelligence gathering run, and there would be a KC-135Q in the vicinity at the end of the flight. To support SR-71 operations from Mildenhall in Suffolk during the 1980s, up to six KC-135Qs could be co-located at any one time, with the tanker aircraft being rotated throughout the SR-71 deployment.

The USAF's tanker fleet has a long association with the 'reconnaissance community' and supported the 'black birds' of the CIA and USAF as well as the 'silver birds' of the larger RB-47 and RC-135 fleet. The Lockheed A-12 was the single-seat precursor of the USAF's more famous SR-71 'Habu'. This A-12, 60-6925, is refuelling from KC-135A 58-0099 during a 1962 test flight. Later operations would be supported by the KC-135Q. (Terry Panopalis Collection)

A familiar photo in aviation books in the 1970s and 1980s was of the sinister black and red form of the SR-71 Habu edging towards the boom of a KC-135Q. The Habus were heavily reliant on tankers, possibly more than any other type in the USAF inventory. (Terry Panopalis Collection)

The KC-135 can be viewed as the basis of an entire generation of Boeing transports, particularly the 707, 727 and 737. It should be noted that the KC-135 and 707 are not the same, despite outward appearances. The Boeing 707 itself went on to become a tanker, especially once airlines began to replace their 707 fleets. Before the term 'tanker/transport' entered the military lexicon, one of the earliest types identified as such was the Boeing 707 Tanker-Transport that Boeing marketed as an excellent use for airline surplus 707s. The prototype aircraft, N792TW, was fitted with a Beech Model 1080 Aerial Refuelling System (ARS) refuelling pod under each wing tip and a camera under the fuselage feeding video to a monitoring station that enabled the flight engineer to observe the refuelling operation. The Royal Australian Air Force (RAAF) converted four of its fleet of six Boeing 707 transports to the tanker/transport role.

Right: To extend the range and endurance of the Lockheed U-2, a refuelling receptacle was added to the U-2C, becoming the U-2F. These were refuelled in trials by Boeing KC-135Q tankers. The main problem with the extra endurance was pilot fatigue. (Terry Panopalis Collection)

Below: Before the term 'tanker/transport' entered the military lexicon, one of the earliest was the Boeing 707 Tanker Transport that Boeing marketed as being an excellent use for airline surplus 707s. The aircraft N792TW was fitted with a Beechcraft Air Refuelling System (ARS) refuelling pod under each wing tip, a camera under the fuselage and a monitoring station that enabled the flight engineer to observe the refuelling operation. (Blue Envoy Collection)

Chapter 4
The Tanker War – Vietnam and Tactical Support

The Boeing KC-135's raison d'être was refuelling SAC's fleet of strategic bombers and reconnaissance aircraft, but that soon changed in the early 1960s with the increase in US operations in South East Asia.

The types involved ranged from the Cessna O-2 Bird Dog to the Lockheed C-5A Galaxy, with tactical air support being provided by aircraft as diverse as the Cessna A-37 Dragonfly and the Boeing B-52. These types had one thing in common – a need for refuelling. Be they the Huns (F-100) and Thuds (F-105) of *Rolling Thunder* from 1965 or the B-52s based in Guam during *Arc Light* and *Linebacker II*, the USAF's KC-135s played a crucial role. Vietnam was the first air war where tankers came to prominence and led to the expression 'No one kicks ass without tanker gas'. A truism if ever there was one. Tankers kept close support types on location, enabled search-and-rescue operations to occur deep inside enemy territory and refuelled transports moving personnel and materiel across the Pacific Ocean and as such were factored into the plans for combat operations. Vietnam set the scene for future tanker operations with air forces around the world.

The forces sent to bases in South Vietnam and Thailand in the early days of US involvement comprised TAC types, including the North American F-100 Super Sabre, McDonnell F-101 Voodoo and Republic F-105 Thunderchief. Oddly enough, early in the post-war era, a TAC/SAC split developed in the USAF, and this was exemplified by refuelling systems, with SAC favouring the flying

In the early days of the Vietnam War, USAF aircraft remained in natural metal. This Republic F-105D Thunderchief is refuelling from a KC-135 fitted with a boom/drogue adapter (BDA), and of note is the curvature of the hose. This curve indicates that the receiver is taking fuel as the receiver must push on the drogue to initiate and maintain fuel flow. The Thunderchief is carrying a pair of AGM-12B Bullpup ASMs and is en route to attack the Thanh Hóa bridge on 3 April 1965. (Terry Panopalis Collection)

As the war in Vietnam escalated, and the USA became more deeply embroiled, tactical aircraft had to be ferried between the USA and South East Asia, meaning tankers worked hard wherever they were. These Republic F-105D Thunderchiefs from the 18TFW are being refuelled using the flying boom by KC-135A 62-3572 near Kadena AFB during 1967. Note that the only stores are wing tanks and a baggage pod on the centreline pylon, suggesting a ferry flight. (Terry Panopalis Collection)

boom for its bombers and TAC preferring the probe-and-drogue for its fighters. As a result, aside from the F-100 Super Sabre, the fighters and strike aircraft of TAC were fitted with both a probe and a receptacle. Air Force Vice Chief of Staff Curtis Le May viewed this state of affairs as counterproductive, and it led to a single tanker force under the control of SAC. To cater for the probe-only machines such as the Super Sabre and Douglas B-66 Destroyer, the BDA was made available to what became a single-type tanker fleet with the type being the KC-135 Stratotanker.

Supporting tactical aircraft became a daily task for the KC-135 force in South East Asia, but especially with the B-52 units operating in the tactical role from Guam during *Arc Light* operations from 1965 and in the 1972 *Linebacker II* campaign. *Arc Light* saw B-52Ds camouflaged (with the TAC SEA scheme, plus black undersides to defeat searchlights) and modified to 'Big Belly' configuration that enabled it to carry up to 70,000lb (31,500kg) of bombs in the battlefield interdiction role. As navigations systems improved, *Arc Light* B-52s could deliver ordnance very close to the friendly troops' front line, making the 'BUFF' one of the weapons most feared by the Viet Cong and North Vietnamese forces.

Boeing's KC-135 Stratotanker supported USAF operations wherever and whenever the Air Force operated. Stratotankers not only refuelled strategic aircraft, bombers and reconnaissance aircraft, but also tactical types such as McDonnell RF-101A Voodoo. Owing to its origin with the USAF's TAC, the RF-101A was fitted for probe and flying boom refuelling, and the type provided key imagery in the Cuban Missile Crisis and the Vietnam War.

Another type reliant on tankers to conduct operations over Vietnam was the Republic F-105 Thunderchief. Like the McDonnell F-101 Voodoo, the Thunderchief had been operated by TAC and was also fitted for drogue and boom refuelling. The Thunderchief carried the burden of USAF air

From 1965 until the end of direct US involvement in Vietnam in 1973, Boeing B-52s operated as very heavy close air support for ground troops during Operation *Arc Light*. In 1972, for Operation *Linebacker II*, the B-52s went into North Vietnam. Operating from Guam, these missions required a great deal of tanker support, especially given the heavy bombloads (up to 70,000lb/31,746kg) in the Big Belly modified B-52s. (Blue Envoy Collection)

The Vietnam War really was a tanker war, with just about every type involved requiring refuelling at some point in an operation. As the North Vietnamese defences improved, support aircraft became key to the success or failure of a mission. Electronic warfare became increasingly important and EW aircraft such as the RB-66C helped protect the strike package from air defences. The B-66, like the F-100 could only refuel from BDA-equipped KC-135s. (Terry Panopalis Collection)

strikes in the early years of the Vietnam War but, as the war progressed, took on specialist roles such as suppression of enemy air defences (SEAD), known as Wild Weasels and armed with AGM-45 Shrike and AGM-78 Standard anti-radiation missiles took on North Vietnamese surface-to-air missile (SAM) radars. USAF strike packages were substantial affairs, comprising fighters to protect the strike aircraft, SEAD types to take on the SAMs/radar-directed anti-aircraft artillery, jammers and pre- and post-operation reconnaissance. Keeping all these in the air required a significant refuelling effort

The Stratotankers refuelled both ends of the spectrum when it came to size. At the opposite end from the Lockheed C-5A Galaxy were the Curtiss A-37 Dragonfly and Northrop F-5C. The USAF conducted trials with the Northrop F-5, a type that was not in USAF service but was being sold abroad to NATO countries such as Canada, Norway and the Netherlands. The US government evaluated the F-5 with the view to using them as fighter-bombers in Vietnam. Officially called the Sparrow Hawk Program, it became better known as Skoshi Tiger. These were F-5Cs: F-5As modified with an in-flight refuelling probe, operated during the USAF's evaluation of lightweight fighters in Vietnam – Skoshi Tiger. 'Skoshi' is a corruption of the Japanese word 'sukoshi' meaning 'small'.

Tankers were also important to the photoreconnaissance capability of the USAF. Boeing's KC-135 Stratotankers not only refuelled strategic aircraft, bombers and reconnaissance aircraft but also tactical reconnaissance types such as McDonnell RF-101A Voodoo 56-0165. Owing to its origin with the USAF's Tactical Air Command, the RF-101A was fitted for probe-and-drogue plus, as seen here, flying boom refuelling, and the type provided key imagery in the Cuban Missile Crisis and the Vietnam War. (Blue Envoy Collection)

Throughout the war in Southeast Asia, hard-working Boeing KC-135s refuelled aircraft as diverse as the Lockheed C-5A Galaxy and the Northrop F-5. These F-5Cs, essentially an F-5A with a refuelling probe, took part in a USAF programme called 'Skoshi Tiger' that assessed the Northrop type's suitability for the Vietnam theatre. The tanker, 57-1349, has been fitted with a BDA to allow it to refuel the F-5Cs. (Blue Envoy Collection)

One area of in-flight refuelling that expanded during the Vietnam War was the refuelling of helicopters. The arrival of powerful gas turbine helicopters, such as the Sikorsky S-61R, enabled the USAF to develop a fast, high-capacity search-and-rescue type such as the HH-3E Jolly Green Giant. Once fitted with a refuelling probe, armour, weapons and a hoist with a jungle penetrator, these could loiter close to a downed airman's position and be refuelled by a Lockheed HC-130P Hercules. The HC-130P Combat King Hercules was fitted with underwing refuelling pods and Fulton recovery gear on the nose. (Blue Envoy Collection)

In-flight refuelling also became crucial to combat search-and-rescue (CSAR) operations that could also become sizeable affairs involving helicopters and close support aircraft. The USAF's rescue units operated Lockheed HC-130P Combat King Hercules as the co-ordination and communications platform for the rescue operation. Some HC-130s were fitted with the Fulton Recovery System to pluck downed aircrew from places where helicopters could not operate. The HC-130s were also fitted with underwing refuelling pods to act as a tanker for the probe-equipped HH-3 and HH-53 helicopters. Later models of the HC-130 were fitted with a refuelling receptacle above the cockpit to allow the Hercules to refuel from KC-135s, thus allowing the Hercules (and any helicopters it in turn refuelled) to remain on station for longer. The facility to act as tanker and receiver has since become a critical aspect of special forces operations, allowing special forces types such as the MC-130J Combat Talon III to penetrate far into enemy territory.

The Vietnam War had shown the importance of tanker support for tactical as well as strategic aircraft. The war in South East Asia had shown that tankers really were force multipliers by keeping USAF aircraft on station longer, penetrating deeper and carrying heavier war loads. The lessons learned in Vietnam were applied in subsequent wars, with tankers becoming highly appreciated assets in any air force's inventory.

The modern equivalent of the HC-130P is the MC-130J Combat Talon III that can act as tanker and receiver (receiver via flying boom, tanker via two under wing HDUs in pods) in its primary role of special forces support. They excel at low flying, as demonstrated in the 'Mach Loop' in north Wales. (Author)

Chapter 5

Reach – USAF Strategic Logistics

Reach has been the callsign of USAF strategic transport aircraft for decades, first as Military Airlift Command (MAC) and since June 1992, Air Mobility Command. The callsign aptly describes American airborne logistics capability and how it extends US influence around the world and how, supported by the largest tanker force in the world, this capacity to move materiel is unsurpassed. Refuelling enabled the US government to transport materiel across the world, even when denied landing or overflight rights, with the prime example being Operation *Nickel Grass*, the resupply of Israel with American weapons in October and November 1973.

The Israeli armed forces took a battering during the October War of 1973, losing a vast number of aircraft and tanks. The US government commenced Operation *Nickel Grass*, which involved airlifting tanks and other equipment direct from the USA. Many European countries refused stopover and refuelling access to US forces, so MAC had to fly direct from the USA, refuelling in-flight. One exception was Portugal, which allowed KC-135s to be based in the Azores to provide refuelling for the transports. Ultimately, a ceasefire was declared before the tanks arrived, but a number of F-4E Phantoms were flown in, direct from USAF stocks. Interestingly, the Phantoms were fitted for boom refuelling and Israeli Aerospace Industries subsequently fitted them with a fixed probe, plumbed into the boom receptacle. A similar situation would arise in 1986 when the USAF faced the withdrawal of overflight rights for Operation *El Dorado Canyon*, the US strikes on Libya.

The KC-135 Stratotanker and the C-135 Stratolifter were the jet-powered workhorses of the USAF's global operations during the 1960s. The Lockheed C-141A StarLifter entered service in 1965 to supplement, and ultimately replace, the Stratolifter, but the C-141A was found to 'bulk out' before it reached its maximum take-off weight. The C-141A was stretched by inserting new fuselage sections

Three types exemplified the Reach callsign in the early 1990s when US airlift capacity was fully committed supporting operations in the Persian Gulf. A McDonnell Douglas KC-10A Extender tanker/transport refuels a Lockheed C-141B while its larger sibling, the C-5B Galaxy, waits its turn for the boom. In-flight refuelling maximised utilisation of transport aircraft enabling take-offs with low fuel weights and avoiding the need for fuel stopovers en route. The latter aspect has led to investigations into the in-flight refuelling of passenger aircraft. (Blue Envoy Collection)

Among the weapon systems rushed across the Atlantic in October 1973 during Operation *Nickel Grass* were additional McDonnell Douglas F-4E Phantoms. These arrived straight from USAF stocks and as such, were fitted with the USAF boom receptacle rather than the retractable probe of the naval Phantoms. After the October War of 1973, a further batch of F-4Es was delivered. Since the Israelis lacked a tanker with boom refuelling, the Phantoms were fitted with a refuelling probe and the necessary pipework to plumb it into the dorsal boom receptacle. (Blue Envoy Collection)

Another problem revealed during the Vietnam War and *Nickel Grass* was that the C-141 bulked out before it reached maximum take-off weight and it could not be refuelled in flight. The C-141A fuselage was stretched to 23ft 4in (7.1m) with plugs either side of the wing box to produce the C-141B. At the same time, a refuelling receptacle was added, increasing its flexibility and strategic value by reducing dependence on refuelling stops. (USAF/DoD)

fore and aft of the wing box to produce the C-141B that was 23ft 4in (7.11m) longer than the C-141A. This much increased its cargo capacity and, to make full use of this and extend its range, a refuelling receptacle was also added, making the C-141B StarLifter an extremely capable transport.

The Vietnam War had worked the KC-135 fleet hard, and yet again the Pacific Ocean had separated the USA from its combat theatre. Moving materiel from the USA to South Vietnam and Thailand (where much of the USAF's tactical air power was based) required a different approach. This led to another tanker project that flew fast enough and high enough to keep pace with the fighters, carried the fuel load to keep the bombers topped up and had the endurance to be in the right place at the right time while providing the logistics support for expeditionary air warfare. The Advanced Tanker Cargo Aircraft was the result of the USAF's experience in Vietnam and Operation *Nickel Grass* and intended to supplement rather than replace the KC-135. Derived from the DC-10-30 airliner, the resulting McDonnell Douglas KC-10 Extender was acquired by the USAF to act as a high-capacity tanker and transport, usually referred to as a tanker/transport. The KC-10 carries its fuel in underfloor tanks, leaving the capacious main cabin free for freight, accessible through a large door on the port side of the forward fuselage. The Extender is fitted with a McDonnell Douglas AARB plus a hose and drogue reel in the rear fuselage. It can also be fitted with two underwing pods known as wing air refuelling pods (WARPs), which means the KC-10 can perform three-point refuelling.

Another benefit of the tanker/transport, specifically the KC-10 Extender, was its ability to use separate fuel tanks for different types of fuel. While this harks back to the KC-97/B-47 with their different fuels, this capability was key to using the KC-10 in support of SR-71 operations in the late 1980s.

Supported by the largest tanker force in the world, the USAF's airlift capacity is exemplified by this Lockheed C-5A Galaxy being refuelled by a Boeing KC-135 Stratotanker. Refuelling enabled the US government to transport materiel across the world even when denied landing or overflight rights, with the prime example being Operation *Nickel Grass*, the resupply of Israel with American weapons in October 1973. (Blue Envoy Collection)

Right: The Extender was fitted with McDonnell Douglas' Advanced Aerial Refuelling Boom (AARB) a variation on the 'flying boom'. The AARB uses digital fly-by-wire controls and features endplates on the 'wings'. The AARB has a much larger performance envelope, including higher speeds. This, plus the Extender's separate fuel tanks, enabled it to refuel aircraft such as the Lockheed SR-71. (Blue Envoy Collection)

Below: The Aeronautica Militare (Italian Air Force) was the launch customer for the Boeing KC-767A Tanker Transport with an order for four examples, while the Japan Air Self-Defence Force also ordered four as the KC-767J. Derived from the Boeing 767-200ER, the KC-767A is fitted with a Boeing High Speed Boom, a centreline HDU in the rear fuselage and wing pods, while the KC-767J for Japan, first delivered in 2008, lacks the HDU in the rear fuselage. This Aeronautica Militare KC-767 Tanker Transport, 14-01, is undergoing predelivery trials and is refuelling USAF B-52H 60-0036 in 2007. (USAF/DoD)

With the KC-135s getting long in the tooth, having first entered service in 1957, and despite the major upgrades, the USAF began to look into a replacement and opted for the tanker/transport option in the shape of the Boeing KC-46 Pegasus, derived from the Boeing KC-767. The launch customer for a tanker derived from the Boeing 767 was the Aeronautica Militare (Italian Air Force) who, followed by the Japan Air Self-Defence Force, ordered four. Named the KC-767 Tanker Transport by Boeing, it was based on the 767-200ER and featured a flying boom, an HDU on the centreline and the facility for underwing pods, thus providing three-point refuelling. The Aeronautica Militare KC-767s entered service with 14° Stormo in 2011 and has supported NATO operations in Afghanistan and Libya.

Although outwardly similar to the KC-767, in being derived from the Boeing 767-200ER, the KC-46 Pegasus is fitted with the wings from the 767-300F. Other modifications include cockpit displays from the Boeing 787 and a modified fly-by-wire AARB from the McDonnell Douglas KC-10. In addition to the new fly-by-wire boom system, the Pegasus is fitted with two wing pods and a centreline installation for an HDU for a drogue system. In reality, with a few exceptions, all the USAF's tankers are tanker/transports, and the USAF has not operated a tanker derived from a bomber.

Another example of how tankers act as force multipliers involves the Rockwell B-1B Lancer, a key component of the post-Cold War USAF and the War on Terror. With its massive weapons load, up to 75,000lb (34,000kg), its ability to refuel from Boeing KC-135s or McDonnell Douglas KC-10 Extenders enabled deep penetration (its original role) of enemy territory or, in the War on Terror, extended loiter over the battlefield with smart weapons to act as close support in Afghanistan. In 1995, a pair of B-1B Lancers repeated the circumnavigation completed by *Lucky Lady II* in 1949. Operation *Coronet Bat* saw two Lancers (Bat 01, 85-0047 *Hellion*, and Bat 02, 85-0082 *Global Power*) fly around the world

A Lockheed F-35A Lightning II from the 461st Flight Test Squadron makes the first contact with a KC-46A Pegasus from the 418th Flight Test Squadron over California in January 2019. To replace the Boeing KC-135s that first entered service in 1957, Boeing proposed the KC-46 Pegasus derived from the Boeing 767-200ER, fitted with the wings from the 767-300F. Other modifications include cockpit displays from the Boeing 787 and a modified AARB from the McDonnell Douglas KC-10. (USAF/DoD)

The Rockwell B-1B Lancer became a key component of the post-Cold War USAF. With its massive weapons load, up to 75,000lb (34,000kg), air-to-air refuelling from Boeing KC-135s as shown here or McDonnell Douglas KC-10 Extenders. The Lancer could conduct deep penetration (its original role) or extended loiter with smart weapons to act as close air support in Afghanistan. Operation *Coronet Bat* demonstrated the USAF's power projection capability with two B-1B lancers circumnavigating the world. Refuelled six times by Boeing KC-135s, the pair of Lancers took 36 hours and 13 minutes to complete their round-the-world mission. (Blue Envoy Collection)

Other examples of the USAF's global reach are the Northrop B-2A Spirit and the McDonnell Douglas KC-10A Extender. B-2s from Whiteman AFB in Missouri, with support from KC-10A Extenders and KC-135R Stratotankers, made a transpacific flight, refuelled five times and delivered ordnance on targets in Afghanistan before recovering to Diego Garcia after 44 hours in the air. One of the B-2s, *Spirit of America*, was 'hot refuelled' at Diego Garcia before returning to Whiteman after running its engines for 72 hours. (Blue Envoy Collection)

dropping ordnance on test ranges as they progressed. The 'Bats' were supported by Boeing KC-135s with six refuellings and returned to Dyess AFB after 36 hours 13 minutes in the air.

Another example of how air-to-air refuelling boosted the USAF's global reach involved the Northrop B-2A Spirit stealth bomber. In October 2001, B-2s from Whiteman AFB in Missouri, with support from McDonnell Douglas KC-10A Extenders and Boeing KC-135R Stratotankers, made a transpacific flight, refuelled five times and delivered ordnance on targets in Afghanistan before recovering to Diego Garcia after 44 hours in the air. One of the B-2s, *Spirit of America*, was 'hot refuelled' at Diego Garcia before returning to Whiteman AFB after running its engines for 72 hours. Thanks to in-flight refuelling, the Pacific is no longer a barrier to American operations.

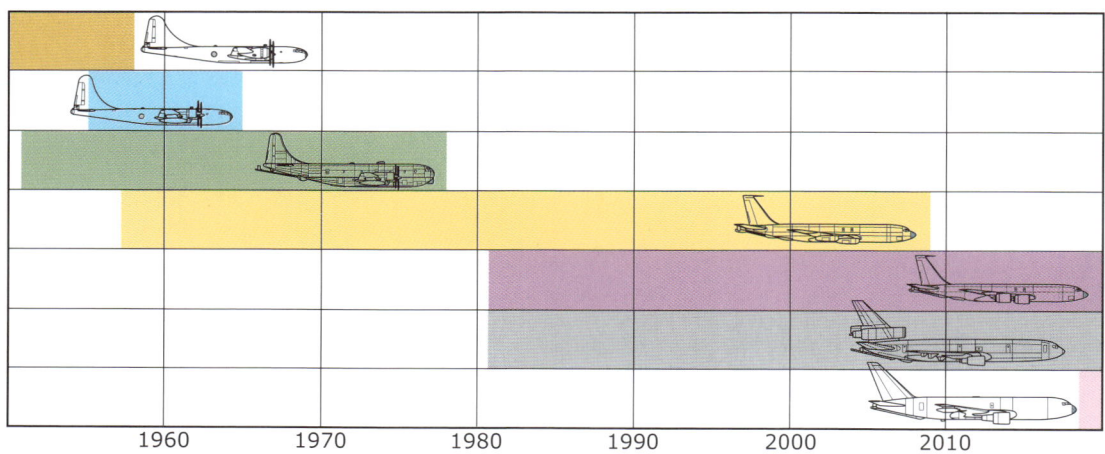

USAF Tanker Timeline – the longevity of the various models of Boeing's KC-135 is evident, and it is expected to serve for decades to come, as is the aircraft it was designed to support: The B-52. (Author)

A Boeing KC-135A refuelling another KC-135A is a rare sight indeed. Converted from former special missions RC-135s or EC-135s, the KC-135s with receptacles, known as refuellable tankers, have been used to support missions such as Operation *Eagle Claw*, the Iranian hostage rescue attempt. Subsequently, all new tanker designs for the USAF, such as the KC-46 Pegasus, have incorporated a refuelling receptacle. (via Robert S Hopkins III)

Chapter 6
Deterrence to Air Defence – RAF Tankers

The RAF has operated a greater variety of tanker aircraft than any other air force, with eight types (including the two Victor K1 and K2 variants) carrying the 'K' mission designator. Like the USAF, the RAF intended using tankers to extend the range of Bomber Command's new V-bombers, but the role was soon widened in to supporting air defence operations in the northeast Atlantic, plus refuelling aircraft on overseas deployments. By the 1970s, the tanker force was mainly involved in air defence support, as the UK's defence commitments became Europe and northeast Atlantic focused. The Falklands Conflict of 1982 gave a foretaste of what was to come after 1989 as British military operations went further afield to Iraq, the Balkans, West Africa and Afghanistan, before returning to Iraq in 2003.

Having conducted trials with Lancasters, Lincolns and Meteors, FRL tried to interest the Air Staff in tankers, but they were somewhat uninterested. That changed when the English Electric Canberra entered service in 1951 with the Air Staff attracted by the prospect of increasing its radius of action with refuelling. After a series of simulated refuellings with Lancaster G-33-2 and a trials Canberra (with no refuelling kit installed) the Air Staff lost interest in early 1952. A year later, conscious of the USAF's successful application of in-flight refuelling, the Air Staff contacted FRL with a proposal to fit probe-and-drogue refuelling equipment to the forthcoming V-bombers, with probes a permanent fixture. The original approach was to use the Valiant as a tanker while maintaining its bombing capability, and they opted to fit the Valiant with underwing refuelling pods, but these lacked the flow rate for large aircraft. The Air Staff decided that an HDU was a better option, but it was to be a removable pack that, along with auxiliary fuel tanks, could be installed in the bomb bay when required.

Even when refuelling, the VC10 must be the most elegant of all aircraft, even in the dark sea grey/dark green camouflage colours applied to ZA141. The Mk.32 pods and the drogue housing for the Mk.17B HDU can be seen here with ZA141 receiving fuel from the centreline hose of its sister ship. The remainder of the VC10 K2 and K3 fleets were finished in the hemp colour scheme. (Blue Envoy Collection)

When the Valiant took on the tanker role it was still in the white anti-flash colour scheme with subdued markings of the V-force strategic bombers. The bomb bay doors are open with the size of the bomb bay tank obvious on Valiant B(K)1 XD820. The FRL Mk.16 HDU was more capable than wing pods for refuelling large aircraft such as Victor B1A (note the Red Steer radome) XH646, which would later become a tanker itself. (Blue Envoy Collection)

Gloster Javelin FAW9 XH965 was operated by the Ministry of Supply and used for trials of the 'lance' refuelling probe. This sturdy item was fitted along the starboard side of the forward fuselage just below the canopy and extended forward to well beyond the radome. Javelin XH965 undertook trials of the installation with the A&AEE's Vickers Valiant B(PR)K1 WX376. The Javelin FAW9F/R was the last in the series, upgraded with the refuelling probe, drop tanks and the AI.17 radar. They served with Fighter Command until 1968. (Blue Envoy Collection)

By 1958, FRL had developed the FRL Mk.16 HDU, which fitted in the bomb bay of the Valiant. As the Vulcan and Victor took on the strategic deterrent role from the Vickers Valiant B1, these were converted to the tanker role, prompting the designation change to B(K)1 or, in the case of the photoreconnaissance capable B(PR)1, the B(PR)K1 tanker.

When the Valiant took on the tanker role, they were still in the white anti-flash colour scheme with toned-down markings of the V-force strategic bombers. To keep the Valiants as viable bombers, the conversions involved fitting an FRL Mk.16 HDU in the bomb bay, and since this was removable and the Valiant could be used for bombing, these became designated B(K)1. Having adopted the HDU, the Valiants became more suitable for refuelling large aircraft such as the Vulcan and Victor, and a total of 44 B(K)1s and 14 B(PR)K1s were converted from B1 and B(PR)1. The Valiant B(K)1 became operational with 214 Squadron in 1958 and 90 Squadron in 1959, with the Valiants in service until December 1964 when fatigue saw the last Valiant grounded and withdrawn.

The Valiant's tanker career was short by modern standards, 1958 to 1965, their retirement prompted by the discovery in mid-1964 of metal fatigue and corrosion in the wing rear spar attachment. A repair programme was initiated in late 1964, but when the Labour government was elected in October 1964, Denis Healey, the newly appointed Defence Secretary, deemed the cost of repairing the fatigued components prohibitive. The Valiant fleet was rapidly withdrawn from service and all examples retired by January 1965.

The replacement for the fatigue stricken Valiants came in the futuristic shape of the Victor B1. As the Blue Steel-capable Victor B2 entered service, and in a nod to the Valiant, Victor B1s were to be converted. However, with the Valiants unexpectedly withdrawn, a somewhat urgent conversion was required; the Victor B1s were to be converted to B(K)1 standard. These were two-point refuellers with an FRL Mk.20A refuelling pod under each wing, and the first of six B(K)1 tankers were delivered to 55 Squadron in late April 1965, commencing operations the following August. While this filled the immediate 'tanker gap', the Victor B(K)1, later called the B1A(K2P), was limited to refuelling fighters. As the conversions programme progressed, more Victor B1 and B1A aircraft were converted to three-point refuellers by installing an FRL Mk.17 HDU in a retractable pallet in the rear fuselage, which FRL describe as a 'pack'. Since they now had no bombing capability, these Victors were designated with the 'K' prefix to become the Victor K1 and K1A, which were operated by 57, 214 and 19 Squadrons.

Handley Page Victor B(K)1 XA918 refuels Avro Vulcan B2 XM648. Of note here is that the Victor retains its white anti-flash finish while the Vulcan has the dark sea grey/dark green camouflage applied when the V-force 'went low level'. With the Vickers Valiants hastily removed from service in January 1965, Handley Page Victor B1As were converted to two-point tankers by fitting an FRL Mk.20A pod under each wing. (Blue Envoy Collection)

While undergoing refuelling trials at the A&AEE during August 1967, Hawker P.1127 (RAF) XV280 (the precursor to the production Harrier GR1) carried out contacts with HP Victor K1 XA918, seen here streaming all three of its hoses to allow the P.1127 to contact each to evaluate flight conditions. Interestingly, these trials led to the Harrier being used in the Transatlantic Air Race of 1969. (Terry Panopalis Collection)

One very important task of the RAF's Victor force in the mid-1960s was the support of overseas deployment of forces 'East of Suez'. These Lightning F6s of 5 Sqn are preparing to refuel from a Victor K1A of 214 Sqn flying over Mount Damavand in Iran. Victors supported deployments to the Middle East and Singapore before UK forces were finally withdrawn in 1971. Tanker operations in the 1960s brought recognition to the role by showing tankers were much more than a means to support strategic bombers.

One very important task of the RAF's tanker force in the mid-1960s was the support of overseas deployment of forces 'East of Suez'. Tanker operations in the 1960s brought recognition to the role by showing tankers were much more than a means to support strategic bombers. The RAF's tankers enabled power projection across a shrinking empire, across areas of the world where landing and staging rights were denied and made the tanker the force multiplier it is today. This would not be lost on other countries.

By the late 1960s, the UK nuclear deterrent had passed to the Blue Steel-armed Vulcan and eventually to the Royal Navy's Polaris boats. Since it was deemed less suited to Strike Command's newly adopted low-level operational role than the Avro Vulcan, the Victor B2 became available for conversion to a tanker. The Victor was most at home at heights above 30,000ft (9,144m) where fighters such as the Lightning and the forthcoming Phantom, optimised for high-altitude operations, typically operated. A total of 24 B2 and B(SR)2 Victors were converted to K2 standard, which included the same Mk.17 pack installation as the Victor K1s. The conversion was undertaken by Hawker Siddeley Manchester owing to Handley Page being barred from tendering for UK government contracts.

Having decided the Victor B2s and SR2s were to be converted to tankers, there arose the not so small matter of who would do the work. Handley Page was effectively banned from tendering for government contracts and had collapsed by the time the contract was let, so the work went to Hawker Siddeley at Woodford. A number of Victors are in various stages of conversion, with Mk.20 refuelling pods in place, in this photo from 1975. Of note are the Nimrods and HS748s in the background. (Avro Heritage via John Harvey)

Air Defence Victors

The change in role from Victor B2 strategic deterrent carrier to K2 tanker coincided with the acceptance into service of the RAF's Phantom FG1 and FGR2 fleet. The Victors would serve one year longer than the Phantoms, and the pairing formed the basis of UK air defences through the 1970s and 1980s. The Victors might have served longer had their fatigue life not been used up by the Falklands Conflict and, towards the end of their career, Operation *Granby* in 1991.

Above: The Victor K2 fleet spent much of its service supporting air defence operations. This Victor K2 of 55 Sqn is refuelling a pair of Lightning F6s from XI Sqn. (Blue Envoy Collection)

Left: Throughout the 1970s and 80s the Victor K2 fleet refuelled the air defence Phantoms of the RAF such as FGR2 XV400 from 29 Sqn at Coningsby. The Phantom is flying 'clean' apart from the 310 imp gal (1,400l) drop tanks on the outboard wing pylons, twin rails for AIM-9 Sidewinders on the inboard wing pylons and what appear to be Sparrow dummy air training missiles (DATM-7) in the forward missile bays. (Blue Envoy Collection)

Whenever RAF early warning radar picked up an unidentified target, an 'X-ray' (an unidentified track that approaches or enters NATO air space), in the UK Air Defence Identification Zone (ADIZ) interceptors on Quick Reaction Alert (QRA) at Leuchars, Leeming or Coningsby would be scrambled to identify and escort the aircraft. At the same time, a Victor tanker would launch from Marham and would keep the interceptors, and any replacements, working in relays to remain on station until the X-ray had left the ADIZ. This has been a long-term commitment for the RAF's tanker forces and continues to this day, with the decade since 2010 being a particularly busy time for the interceptors and tankers. Over the years, only the aircraft have changed.

Right: The reason the RAF's focus changed to the northeast Atlantic was the threat to NATO naval operations posed by Soviet maritime aircraft such as the Tupolev Tu-95 'Bear-D' that provided over-the-horizon targeting for Soviet naval units. These were escorted by RAF Phantoms such as FG1 XV574 of 43 Sqn at Leuchars. The Victor tankers enabled the Phantoms to operate in the GIUK Gap. (Terry Panopalis Collection)

Below: A familiar scene in the 1970s as a 57 Sqn Victor K2 refuels a 29 Sqn Phantom from Coningsby. Such air defence operations stretched the tanker and interceptor forces, while the need to conduct barrier air patrols in the GIUK Gap in a time of hostilities prompted ASR395 for a long-range anti-bomber aircraft that led to the development of the Tornado ADV and ASR406, leading to the development of the VC10 tankers. These were in hand when the balloon went up 'Down South' (Terry Panopalis Collection)

Air-to-Air Refuelling Aircraft

In 1975, a new deployment task arose from a need for a British armed forces presence in Central America. To guard against any threat to Belize from neighbouring Guatemala, the British government deployed an independent flight of Harriers: Hardet Belize (Harrier Detachment, Belize) and later, No. 1417 Flight, to Belize City's airport. Vickers VC10 C1 transports were tasked with logistics support for the deployment of the Harrier GR3s, while Handley Page Victor K2s provided refuelling on the transatlantic ferry flights. The need for two separate aircraft fulfilling different roles influenced

Left: The distances involved in operating around the Falkland Islands and South Georgia are staggering. On a comparative scale, the Falklands are as far from London as Singapore and the distance is one third of the polar circumference of the Earth. Operating over the ocean for such distances required lots of tankers, SAR support plus exceptional navigation and flying.

Below: Hardet Belize, and later No. 1417 Flight, in Belize comprised Harrier GR3s. Their deployment required Vickers VC10 C1 transports for logistics support, while Handley Page Victor K2s provided refuelling on the transatlantic ferry flights. This led to the drawing up of Staff Target AST411 for a 'Supertanker'. (Terry Panopalis Collection)

the Air Staff's thinking and led in 1981 to the drawing up of Air Staff Target AST411 for a single dual-role aircraft. At the time of its drafting, the two-role aircraft was not viewed as a necessity, but mainly something to examine for the future. All that changed in April 1982 when some scrap merchants landed on a remote island in the South Atlantic; tankers became more important than ever.

The Victor K2 fleet provided sterling service in the Falklands Conflict, supporting Vulcan and Hercules operations from the 'forward' base at Ascension Island, a volcanic island 3,300nm (6,100km) from the Falklands, essentially halfway from the UK. Victor K2s also provided long-range photoreconnaissance using F95 cameras mounted in the former bomb aimer's position to provide imagery of the Falkland Islands and South Georgia. The Victor's swansong came in the 1991 Gulf War during Operation *Granby*, when they refuelled not only RAF aircraft but other coalition aircraft, especially US Navy types. Having worked hard in the South Atlantic, and subsequently in the Gulf, the Victors were low on fatigue life and therefore withdrawn in 1993. The Victor outlived its V-bomber contemporaries, and if ever an aircraft could be described as futuristic, it is the Victor. Its like will not be seen again.

Falklands Fallout

Having concentrated on the northwest European/east Atlantic theatre for a decade, topping up Lightnings and Phantoms intercepting 'Bears' and 'Badgers', the 1982 Falklands Conflict, especially the tempo of operations, placed a heavy burden on the RAF's Victor K2 force. Operations in the South Atlantic required long over-water flights, prompting existing types that had no refuelling capability to be fitted with refuelling probes. The onset of hostilities prompted trips to aviation museums to strip refuelling kit from recently retired exhibits, especially Avro Vulcans. The salvaged probes were fitted to newly refurbished Nimrod MR2s to produce the MR2P, with 'P' standing for 'Probe'. The certification trials were conducted in quick time, with Nimrod MR2P XV238 undertaking trials at the Aircraft and Armament Experimental Establishment (A&AEE), making multiple contacts, dry and wet, with HP Victor K2 XH672 acting as tanker. The probe's installation had an adverse effect on the Nimrod's directional stability, a situation remedied by the addition of a ventral strake on the rear fuselage and finlets at mid-span on the tailplanes.

Operations in the South Atlantic required long oceanic flights, prompting existing types to be fitted with refuelling probes. Hawker Siddeley Nimrod MR2s were fitted with probes to become MR2P with trials of the installation being undertaken by Nimrod XV238 making multiple contacts, dry and wet, with Handley Page Victor K2 XH672. (Blue Envoy Collection)

The installation proved successful and entered service, with the first probe-equipped Nimrod arriving at Ascension's Wideawake Airfield on 7 May to provide anti-submarine and search-and-rescue cover for the task force. One anti-submarine sortie required 18 refuellings from Victor tankers. The probe would become a permanent fixture on the entire Nimrod MR2 fleet and the kit was added to the R1 ELINT variant. Originally intended as a temporary installation, the in-flight refuelling kit would prove to be the Nimrod's undoing, but that was 24 years in the future and in a different kind of war.

Following Victor

The Falklands Conflict showed how important air-to-air refuelling was to conducting modern warfare but also showed the limitations of converting bombers to the role. A new tanker was already in the offing in the shape of the VC10, but something with a bit more capability was required, leading to the Supertanker.

In the aftermath of the Falklands Conflict of 1982, while awaiting new tanker aircraft, the RAF operated another two tankers that were rather hurried conversions of existing types. The first was the Avro Vulcan B2, which was fitted with three 995 imp gal (4,523l) fuel tanks in the bomb bay and a Mk.17 HDU pack, as used on the Victor, installed in the tail cone ECM bay with a new fairing added under the tail cone to house the drogue basket. The six Vulcan B2s converted, designated Vulcan K2, were intended to support air defence operations in the UK, plugging the 'tanker gap' created by the greatly increased workload on the Victor force until arrival of the VC10 K2s, thus freeing up Victors for operations 'down south' on Ascension Island.

In addition to the new fairing under the tail cone, and three auxiliary tanks in the bomb bay, the six Vulcan K2s gained new markings on the underside to help the receiver line up for contact. This included a

Vulcan K2 XH560, formerly a maritime radar reconnaissance (MRR) platform that had been fitted with air sampling pods in the 1970s, gained a new lease of life as a tanker. The conversion involved new drogue housing under the tail cone, a neater solution, with more fuel capacity, than a Valiant-style bomb bay installation. (Terry Panopalis Collection)

The Vulcan K2 refuelling installation comprised an FRL Mk.17 HDU in the former ECM equipment bay plus a housing for the drogue with status lights on the sides. Of note in this image is how the drogue basket has compressed to fit into the housing. (Terry Panopalis Collection)

Trials with the Vulcan K2 prompted the addition of new paintwork to improve the visibility of the drogue during refuelling operations. The scheme replaced the camouflage on the underside of the wings with white paint applied from wing tip to wing tip and forward between the engines to the front edge of the bomb bay. DayGlo alignment stripes were then applied to the drogue housing and either side of the centreline. (Terry Panopalis Collection)

large expanse of white across the entire span of the rear portion of the wings and between the engine nacelles to the forward edge of the bomb bay doors. DayGlo alignment markings were applied on the white area forward of the HDU housing. The conversion of the Vulcan B2 to K2 was a success and took the pressure off the Victor K2 fleet by operating from late June 1982 until March 1984. The Vulcan K2s were withdrawn as the workload on the Victor fleet lessened and VC10 K2s became available in the summer of 1984.

The distances involved in supporting British Forces in the Falkland Islands were compounded by the lack of a runway suitable for large aircraft at Port Stanley. This made the Hercules C1 the ideal choice for the air bridge, and although the type could operate from Port Stanley, it lacked the range for the Ascension–Falklands leg and did not possess an in-flight refuelling capability. The initial solution was to fit 25 Hercules C1s with refuelling probes, becoming Hercules C1Ps, which made for entertaining refuelling from Victor K2s in a shallow dive, described at the time as 'toboggan runs'.

One suggestion to make refuelling between Victor and Hercules less dramatic was 'inverse refuelling', a technique that had been suggested for the RAF's putative E-2K Hawkeye fleet in the 1970s. The method involved the receiver carrying a buddy pack (or even an HDU) and flying ahead and above the tanker. The receiver streamed the hose/drogue, and the tanker made contact with the drogue. Once the green lights lit up, the tanker pumped fuel through its probe, up the hose and into the receiver.

The ultimate solution was to convert six Hercules C1s to the C1(K) by fitting them with two or four auxiliary fuel tanks (overload tanks from the Hawker Siddeley Andover C1) secured in the cargo bay and an FRL Mk.17 HDU pack mounted in a frame on the inside of the cargo ramp. For the conversion to the tanker role, the ramp was sealed shut and fitted with an external fairing to house the drogue. The HDU drew its supply from the wing tanks, rather than tanks in the cargo hold. Interestingly, the Hercules C1(K) was the first RAF tanker to enter service that was not based on a bomber.

Tanker refuelling tanker had always been possible but became of supreme importance in supporting operations 6,888nm (12,750km) from the UK in the South Atlantic, most famously in support of the Operation *Black Buck* raids on Port Stanley, each involving around 15 Victor sorties and 18 refuellings. Tankers were also important in support of Hercules C1Ps delivering urgently required spares and other kit to the fleet and land forces, even delivering personnel by parachute to ships in the South Atlantic. To put one Vulcan on target, a Nimrod on station or a Hercules delivery required up to five Victors, most of which refuelled other Victors. In essence, it meant that the fuel burned in the Hercules' engines had been 'through' four separate Victors!

A 57 Sqn Victor K2 refuels a 55 Sqn K2 in what would become a common practice during the recovery of the Falklands. Tankers were crucial to the RAF's operations in the South Atlantic and to put one Nimrod on station over the Task Force required up to five Victors, most of which refuelled other Victors. (Blue Envoy Collection)

Having had the refuelling equipment installed, the Hercules C1K underwent trials at the Aircraft & Armament Experimental Establishment (A&AEE), which involved contacts and refuellings between the A&AEE's Phantom FG1, XT597, and Hercules C1K, XV201. The Hercules C1K would support Phantom operations in the Falklands from 1983. (Terry Panopalis Collection)

In addition to supporting the air bridge to the Falkland Islands, one of the tasks for the Hercules C1K tanker conversion was support of No. 1435 Flight. Phantom FGR2s replaced Hawker Siddeley Harrier GR3s in 1983 and operated as the islands' primary air defence from RAF Port Stanley (Port Stanley Airport) from 1983 until RAF Mount Pleasant was completed in 1985. Prior to Mount Pleasant opening, the runway at Port Stanley had been extended using pierced steel planking and a portable arrestor system installed to allow the Phantoms to make arrested landings. The Phantoms were themselves replaced by Panavia Tornado F3s in 1992, with Typhoon FGR4s taking on the role in 2009.

VC10 – A Real Lost Opportunity

After a somewhat protracted procurement process, the first of 14 VC10 C1 strategic transports was delivered to the RAF in 1965. From 1960, Vickers had been actively marketing the VC10 as a multi-role military aircraft with a number of variants including maritime reconnaissance, deterrent carrier, airborne early warning and in-flight refuelling tanker. This last proposal was a three-point tanker that carried a Mk.17 HDU in the lower rear freight hold, forward of the engines. The hold's door on the port side of the fuselage was to be replaced by an external fairing that acted as a hose guide and a housing for the drogue basket when the hose was hauled in. A Mk.20 pod was to be fitted in each wing tip or on the outboard pylons that had been designed to carry Skybolt air-launched ballistic missiles. Later VC10 tanker studies were fitted with an HDU on the centreline of the tail cone, with the drogue deployed through the open doors of an access hatch. Unfortunately, the RAF showed little or no interest in the VC10 tankers, there being plenty of surplus Victors to convert, and it would be 1977 before the VC10 would be considered again when the need for additional tankers was recognised. Support for the Tornado Air Defence Variant (ADV) and Nimrod airborne early warning (AEW) operations in the Greenland/Iceland/UK Gap needed more tanker support, which prompted the issue of Air Staff Requirement ASR406 that called for the conversion of airline surplus VC10s into tankers.

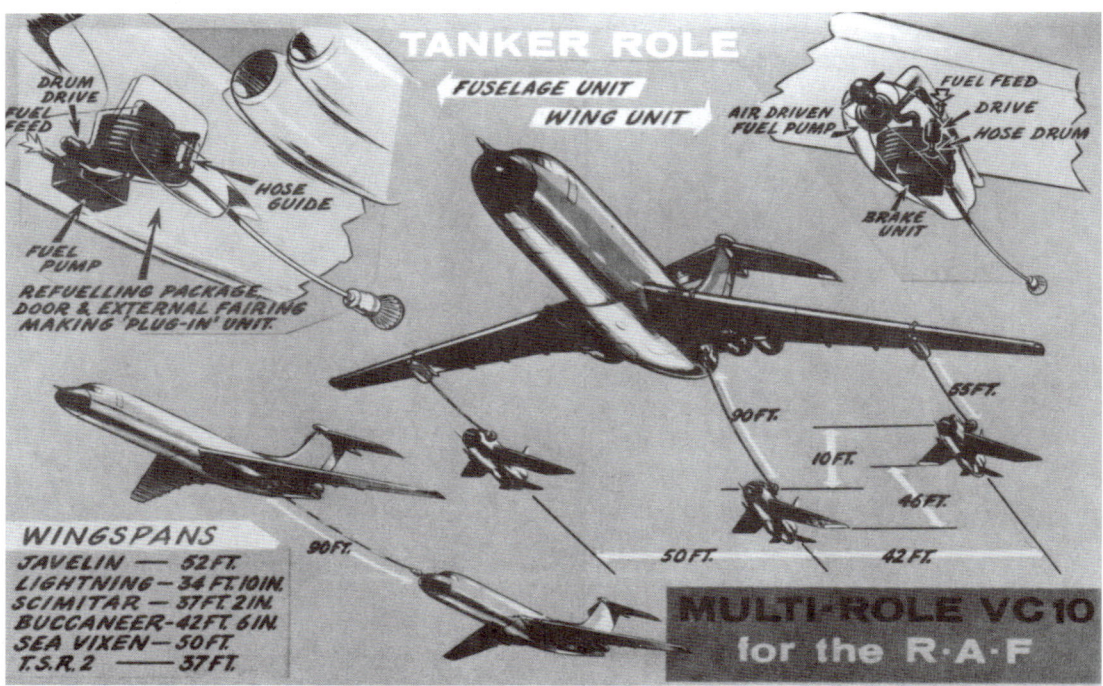

Above: Proposals for a VC10 tanker pre-date 1977's AST406 by more than a decade. In January 1964, Vickers presented the Air Staff with a brochure for a three-point tanker version of the VC10 as part of its multi-role VC10 study. In addition to wing pods, an HDU would be fitted in the VC10 rear baggage hold, and the hose would be fed out of the port side via a fairing that would replace the hold's hatch and house the drogue. (Brooklands Museum)

Left: Prior to their retirement in 1988, Lightnings such as F6 XR771 were regular users of tankers such as this 101 Sqn VC10 K3. The somewhat spindly refuelling probe was first fitted on the F1A and enabled an interceptor designed for use over the North Sea to range further afield. (Blue Envoy Collection)

The VC10 K2 as it had been intended – refuelling Tornado ADVs. Lit by a low sun, the VC10 passes fuel to a pair of Tornado F3s. Interestingly, these F3s are carrying stores on their outboard wing pylons with a Phimat chaff dispenser on the starboard and BOZ-107 chaff and flare dispenser to port. (Terry Panopalis Collection)

Of course, being highly flexible, VC10 tankers were not only an air defence asset. Support for ground attack types such as the Tornado GR1 and Harrier GR3 was also important, particularly on deployments. These Harrier GR3s are fitted with the fixed, bolt-on probe while refuelling from VC10 K3 ZA149. (Terry Panopalis Collection)

The outcome of Air Staff Requirement ASR406 was that the VC10 K2 that was to support air defence operations by Phantoms, such as 43 Squadron's FG1s operating from Leuchars, and their replacement from 1989, the Tornado ADV. The VC10 K2s were fitted with underwing Mk.32 refuelling pods and a Mk.17 HDU in a modified bay in the rear fuselage, with the K2 and K3 having fuel tanks fitted in the cabin. The subsequent issue of ASR415 resulted in four airline surplus Super VC10s being converted to K3 tankers with fuel tanks on the main deck, while a further five Super VC10s became K4 tanker/transports that kept the entire cabin available for freight.

On the retirement of the Victor, VC10s such as this K3 became the primary tanker for the RAF's air defences. Another task for the VC10, such as ZA149, was refuelling trials for the Eurofighter 2000 programme, with ZH588 making contacts, wet and dry. (Blue Envoy Collection)

The first Vickers VC10 K2 delivered was ZA141, which came out of the BAC Filton plant resplendent in a dark green and dark sea grey over a light aircraft grey camouflage scheme. The only example to carry these colours, ZA141 reverted to the same hemp overall scheme as the later tanker VC10s at its first major maintenance visit. By the early 1980s, RAF aircraft were being repainted in hemp and later, Barley Grey, the colour named after the chap who developed it.

The outcome of ASR406 was that the VC10 K2 that was to support air defence operations by Phantoms, such as 43 Squadron FG1, XV577, from 1989, the Tornado Air Defence Variant. The first Vickers VC10 K2 delivered was ZA141, which came out of the BAC Filton plant, resplendent in a dark green and dark sea grey over a light aircraft grey camouflage scheme. (Terry Panopalis Collection)

Supertanker

In 1975, the USAF carried out a series of trials under the title Advanced Tanker Cargo Aircraft, a requirement for what became known as a tanker/transport. The USAF, in 1977, selected the DC-10-30CF as the basis for the KC-10 Extender, and this entered service in March 1981.

The lessons learnt from supporting an army on the other side of the world in Vietnam and Operation *Nickel Grass* led to the Advanced Tanker Cargo Aircraft Program. The resulting McDonnell Douglas KC-10 Extender tanker/transport was fitted with McDonnell Douglas' AARB, which through an active control system with digital fly-by-wire controls offered larger disconnect and control envelopes when compared with Boeing's flying boom. The KC-10 Extender was also fitted with an HDU for probe-equipped receivers and this flexibility, plus its large fuel and cargo capacity, made the Extender a true force multiplier. The Extender set the trend for other air forces to adopt the tanker/transport based on wide-bodied, big-fan airliners, and the RAF aimed to follow suit, so the Air Staff drew up ASR411. In response, BAe at Woodford drew up proposals for tanker/transports – known to BAe Woodford as the 'Supertanker' – such as the BAe.836 based on the Airbus A300C4 and the BAe.843 derived from the A300B. The BAe.844 stemmed from the A310 and was to be a multi-role type that included AEW in its repertoire to produce a true force multiplier.

Above: The RAF had plans for a 'Supertanker' along the same lines as the USAF's KC-10 Extender, but despite showing interest in ex-Laker Airways DC-10s, the RAF received the Lockheed L.1011-500 TriStar. TriStar K1 ZD951 in Barley Grey scheme rotates on take-off. TriStar tankers may return to the skies as 'tankers for hire'. (MOD/Open Government Licence)

Right: The largest aircraft type acquired in the fallout from the Falklands Conflict was the Lockheed L-1011-500 TriStar. TriStars operated the UK–Ascension–Falklands air bridge for many years as well as supporting Tornado F3 operations in the GIUK Gap, as demonstrated by TriStar K1 ZD951. (Blue Envoy Collection)

The largest aircraft type acquired by the RAF in the fallout from the Falklands Conflict was the Lockheed L-1011-500 TriStar. In 1981, the Air Staff had written requirement ASR411 for a tanker/transport along the same lines as the USAF's KC-10 Extenders but lacked the funds for their 'Supertanker'. Post-Falklands, and with a garrison operation to support, the tanker/transport was a priority with mothballed former Laker Airways DC-10-10s and DC-10-30s viewed as the best solution. Her Majesty's government had other ideas and took six Lockheed L-1011-500 Tristars off the hands of a cash-strapped British Airways and a further three from Pan Am.

The TriStars were converted to tanker/transports by Marshalls of Cambridge with two K1s as dedicated tankers (but with some cargo/passenger capacity), four as KC1 tanker/transports and three as C2/C2A transports. The K1s and KC1s were fitted with two fuel tanks in the underfloor baggage holds and aside from the original two TriStar K1s with a single HDU. The TriStar tankers were fitted with two FRL Mk.17T HDUs in the rear fuselage with the refuelling process monitored via CCTV from the flight engineer's workstation. The cameras were installed in the small turret fitted on the centreline, forward of the drogue fairings, and enabled the operator to view the receiver throughout the contact. Despite having two HDUs, the TriStars were effectively single-point tankers, as there was little or no separation between the drogue units.

The TriStars operated the UK–Ascension–Falklands air bridge for many years as well as supporting Tornado F3 operations in the Greenland–Iceland–UK (GIUK) Gap, but in the post-Cold War world the TriStars soon became the long-range workhorses of the RAF. Wherever British forces operated, the TriStars were found whether it be the Falklands air bridge or topping up US Navy Hornets over Afghanistan, the RAF certainly got their money's worth with the TriStar.

In addition to the air bridge to the South Atlantic, TriStars were also operated by No. 1312 Flight from RAF Mount Pleasant in the Falkland Islands in support of the Eurofighter Typhoon FGR4s of

As the different variants of TriStar entered service, they had to undertake refuelling trials at the A&AEE. TriStar KC1, ZD950, refuelled Hercules C1P XV210 in one such trial. (Terry Panopalis Collection)

The RAF also refuelled US probe-equipped types such as these US Navy Paveway-armed McDonnell Douglas F/A-18C Hornets refuelling from 206 Sqn Lockheed TriStar K1 ZD951 high over Afghanistan in 2008. Tristar K1 ZD951 was the last TriStar flown by the RAF when it flew into retirement in 2014. (Terry Panopalis Collection)

Wideawake Airfield on Ascension Island became a staging post for RAF operations in the Falklands Conflict and has remained so since. Wideawake was by the mid-1980s hosting the range of RAF tankers including Hercules C1K, TriStar KC1 and Victor K2. (Blue Envoy Collection)

No. 1435 Flight. The TriStars only operated from August 2013, when the VC10s were withdrawn, until February 2014 when an Airbus Voyager arrived in the Falklands.

The arrival of the Lockheed TriStar gave the RAF the boost in capability it needed to support the Falklands garrison and, post-1989, the expansion of British operations around the world. The nine TriStars began entering service with 216 Squadron in 1984 and served until 2014, with ZD950 making the last flight of an RAF TriStar when it entered storage at Bruntingthorpe in Leicestershire.

After yet another war, this time Operation *Granby*/First Gulf War in 1991, additional refuelling capability was required, and in the early 1990s ASR416 was issued to cover the conversion of the remaining 13 Vickers VC10 C1 transports to C1K two-point tanker/transports. The conversion involved fitting FRL Mk.32 pods under the outer wings and a CCTV monitoring system. The entire C1 fleet was converted to C1K standard, and all retained their original passenger/cargo capacity, meaning they could provide transport and refuelling for operations such as overseas deployments of RAF squadrons, known as 'drags' by the USAF.

Conversion of surplus airliners to tanker/transports was not a solely British pursuit, as the Royal Netherlands Air Force (RNLAF) acquired three McDonnell Douglas KDC-10s. Two former Martinair DC-10-30Fs were converted to tankers and entered service in 1995. After one crashed, a third DC-10-30F was acquired and converted. KDC-10s operated in support of RNLAF and NATO operations, and in late 2020, were in the process of being replaced by the Airbus A330 MRTT (Multi-Role Tanker Transport), with one KDC-10 sold to Omega Aerial Refuelling Services, a private refuelling contractor.

The need for more tankers in the 1990s prompted the fitting of FRL Mk.32 wing pods to the VC10 C1 fleet to become C1K, such as XV109. These retained their transport capability while providing tanker support for types such as the Tornado F3. (Terry Panopalis Collection)

Chapter 7
Private Practice

The RAF's TriStar and VC10 replacement was outlined in the 1997 Future Strategic Tanker Aircraft (FSTA) requirement and under the then-current government policy, FSTA was to be acquired through a private finance initiative. This was a contract whereby the RAF rented its tanker capacity from a private company, with AirTanker plc winning the contract with the Airbus A330 MRTT, designated 'Voyager' by the RAF. Three variants of the Voyager serve with the RAF: the KC2 with underwing pods and the KC3 with wing pods and an HDU in the rear fuselage. The third variant is the VIP-configured KC2 ZZ336. There was no KC1, but that may have been reserved for a standard boom-equipped A330 MRTT.

A total of 14 Voyagers were acquired, with three KC2s (one of these, ZZ343, was part of the 'Surge Fleet') fitted with Cobham 805E Fuselage Refuelling Unit (FRU, the new name for an HDU) in the rear fuselage, and seven KC3s with an FRU and a Cobham 905E under each outer wing to provide three-point refuelling. A single Voyager KC3 (ZZ336) has been converted to VIP transport, complete with special colour scheme, but has retained its refuelling capability and has been operated on widely publicised operations supporting Typhoons intercepting Russian aircraft in the UK ADIZ. A further

Changing of the guard. After almost 30 years' service with the RAF as a tanker, and 48 years as a transport, the Vickers VC10 bowed out in 2014, replaced by the Airbus A330 Voyager. In recognition of this, VC10 K3 ZA150 flew in formation with Voyager KC2 ZZ331. (MOD/Open Government Licence)

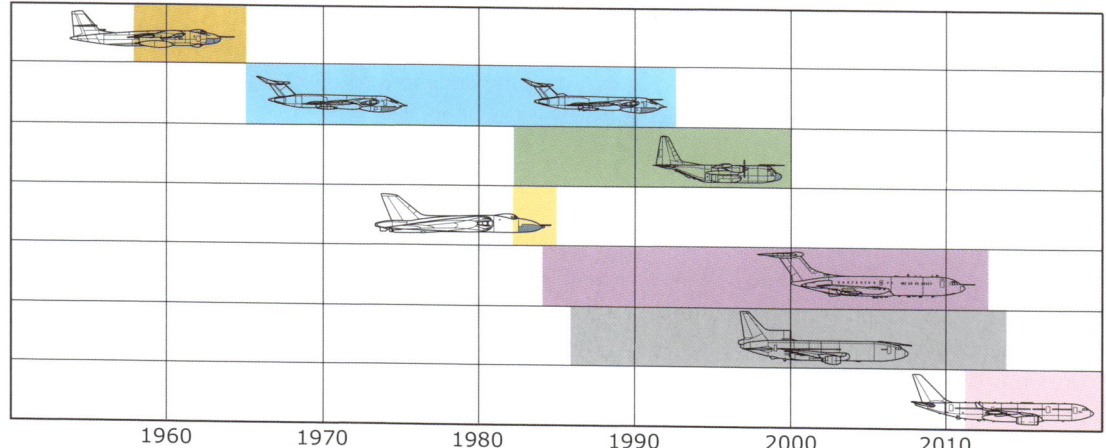

The RAF has fielded seven types of tanker (eight if the Victor K1 and K2 are considered as separate types) with four distinct types in service at one point in the early 1990s. (Author)

four 'demodified' Airbus A330-243s form a surge fleet that AirTanker uses to generate revenue, for example by Thomas Cook Airlines for holiday charter flights. AirTanker also operates the Falkland Islands air bridge, refuelling at Ascension (or Dakar in Senegal if Ascension is unavailable). The surge fleet can be converted, like ZZ343, back to full tanker capability if required.

Tankers for Hire

Tankers for hire has become a fixture in the world of military contracting, enabling air forces that lack the capability to move their aircraft around the world for exercises or operational deployments that would have required refuelling stops. One bizarre aspect of this was the purchase of a Ukrainian Il-78 'Midas' by an American company for commercial refuelling operations. As of 2020, the 'Midas' was undergoing refurbishment in the USA.

Omega Aerial Refuelling Services was founded in 2004 and operated the Boeing KC-707, such as N707MQ, which is performing the first air-to-air refuelling of a UAV, a Northrop Grumman X-47B. The company has expanded in recent years, providing refuelling on a contract or ad hoc basis. (US Navy/DoD)

To fill the refuelling gap produced by the ramping up of military operations at the turn of the century, Omega Aerial Refuelling Services was founded in 2004. Omega operated the Boeing KC-707, such as N707MQ (famed for performing the first air-to-air refuelling of an uninhabited air vehicle (UAV), a Northrop Grumman X-47B) but has since increased its fleet to meet demand from air forces around the world. The Omega fleet expansion included three Boeing KC-707s and two McDonnell Douglas KDC-10s the company purchased from the RNLAF when these were replaced by Airbus A330 MRTTs. Omega has supported the RAF, RAAF and Royal Canadian Air Force (RCAF) operations when extra capacity was required.

Another type earmarked for the contract refuelling market was the Lockheed TriStar, specifically the former RAF KC1. Tempus Applied Solutions bought six TriStars, four KC1s and two C2s with the intention of restoring three of the KC1s into service while using the fourth KC1 and the two C2s for spares. Then, in 2020, a proposal emerged to reactivate former RAF VC10s and return them to service as contract tankers. Kepler Aerospace, working with GJD Services Ltd (also involved in the TriStar deal) examined VC10 K3 ZA150 stored in taxiable condition at Dunsfold and became interested in two examples, K3 ZA147 and K4 ZD241, stored at Bruntingthorpe. Perhaps the 'Queen of the Skies' will fly again?

Airbus's first foray into in-flight refuelling, the A310 MRTT was an A310 airliner fitted with two underwing FRL Mk32B-900 pods, five underfloor fuel tanks, a large cargo door on the port forward fuselage and a Fuel Operator Station. The A310 MRTT first flew in 2003 and has since entered service with the Luftwaffe and, in its CC-150 Polaris guise, the RCAF, to meet a requirement to ferry four CF-188 Hornets across the Atlantic. The A310 MRTT offers a fuel offload capacity on a par with the Boeing KC-135 plus the cargo capacity of 36 tons (37 tonnes) or up to 214 passengers. Interestingly, BAe in 1982 had proposed such a conversion as the BAe.844, but the MOD opted for second-hand Lockheed TriStars.

Airbus's first foray into in-flight refuelling, the A310 MRTT was a conversion of the A310 airliner, fitted with two underwing FRL Mk32B-900 pods and four additional fuel tanks. Royal Canadian Air Force CF-188 Hornets 188770 and 18874 await refuelling from Airbus CC-150 Polaris 15004. (RCAF)

Airbus has conducted a great deal of research into air-to-air refuelling and has undertaken trials of an automatic refuelling system for the A330 MRTT. The system, used with the Airbus Aerial Refuelling Boom System (ARBS), uses pattern recognition to identify the receiver aircraft and its refuelling receptacle before 'flying' the boom into the receptacle. Airbus calls the system A3R (automatic air-to-air refuelling) and conducted trials over the Atlantic with a Portuguese Air Force F-16. The first customer will be the Republic of Singapore Air Force as an upgrade to its A330 MRTT fleet.

Like all A330 MRTTs (apart from the RAF's Voyagers) the RAAF's 33 Sqn Airbus KC-30As carry two Cobham 905E underwing refuelling pods plus the AARBS to refuel large aircraft. This promotes inter-service tasking and enables the RAAF to operate alongside air forces in the Far East such as the Republic of Singapore Air Force (another A330 MRTT operator) that use US equipment including F-15 eagles and F-16 Fighting Falcons and, of course, the USAF.

Normally kept in the background while the fast jets hog the limelight, the RAF's Voyagers hit the headlines in 2020. Heavily criticised in the popular press for having an expensive paint job, Voyager KC2 ZZ336 was repainted during routine deep maintenance. The aircraft is to be used to transport Her Majesty The Queen, her Prime Minister, staff and press corps on overseas visits while retaining its operational tanker role. Its sorties into the northeast Atlantic supporting QRA missions produce a steady stream of press releases. This author can't wait to see a snap of ZZ336 flying in formation with a 'Bear'!

Airbus's A3R underwent trials with a Portuguese Air Force F-16. This image shows the symbology employed and how the system recognises the aircraft and the boom. Once within the refuelling envelope, the software identifies the location of the refuelling receptacle and guides the boom nozzle into it. (Airbus)

Like all A330 MRTTs (apart from the RAF's Voyager), the Royal Australian Air Force's 33 Sqn Airbus KC-30As are fitted with a boom system to refuel large aircraft such as the USAF Boeing B-1B Lancer. This improves inter-service operations and enables the RAAF to operate alongside services in the Far East such as the Republic of Singapore Air Force (another A330 MRTT operator) that use US equipment. (Commonwealth of Australia)

Despite criticism in the popular press for its expensive paint job, Voyager KC2 ZZ336 was repainted during routine deep maintenance. In addition to its VIP role, known as *Vespina* tasking, ZZ336 operates as a tanker in support of RAF operations and is shown on a photoshoot with two Lockheed Lightnings from 617 Sqn and a Typhoon FGR4. (MOD/Open Government Licence)

Boom Time?

The first aircraft in RAF service fitted with a boom receptacle was the Sentry AEW1, but it is also fitted with refuelling probes, offset to starboard due to the retention of the boom refuelling receptacle on the aircraft's centreline above the cockpit. The Sentry is the only aircraft in the RAF inventory capable of refuelling with either the probe-and-drogue or flying boom systems. The RAF's Voyagers (operated by AirTanker plc) were ordered without a flying boom, which could be perceived as short-sighted, as the Boeing P-8A Poseidon MRA1, RC-135W AirSeeker R1 and the forthcoming Wedgetail AEW1 all have refuelling receptacles. Another, possibly favourable, outcome from fitting the Voyagers with booms could be that it would enable off-the-shelf F-35As to be acquired rather than additional, more expensive F-35Bs.

Realistically, aside from the F-35, none of these US types were envisaged for RAF service when FSTA was drawn up and bid for. Fitting the Voyagers with booms has apparently been under discussion, but no decision has been made as of the end of 2020. The RAF's new surveillance types will need to rely on allies for their refuelling needs. Interestingly, the RAF does not refuel its fleet of Boeing C-17 Globemaster IIIs in flight, not for any practical reason, merely because none could be spared from their operational schedule for the necessary clearance programme.

The RAF's Boeing E-3D Sentry AEW1 fleet is fitted with a refuelling probe in addition to the boom receptacle of the original Sentries used by the USAF and NATO. With the increasing number of US types entering RAF service in the support role, being restricted to flying boom refuelling will have an impact on their operational flexibility, unless the Voyager fleet is fitted with flying booms. (Blue Envoy Collection)

Chapter 8
Rotary Refuelling – Helicopters

As noted above, one area of in-flight refuelling that expanded during the Vietnam War was the refuelling of helicopters. The arrival of gas turbine-powered helicopters such as the Sikorsky S-61R enabled the USAF to develop a fast high-capacity search-and-rescue type such as the HH-3E Jolly Green Giant. Once fitted with a refuelling probe, armour, weapons and a hoist with a jungle penetrator, these could loiter close to a downed airman's position and be refuelled by a Lockheed HC-130P Hercules. The HC-130P Combat King Hercules, fitted with underwing refuelling pods, could provide refuelling and on-site co-ordination for the rescue operation.

Since the mid-1960s, and using techniques developed during the Vietnam War, recovery of downed aircrew and infiltration/exfiltration of special forces has become an increasingly important role for helicopters, with in-flight refuelling playing a major part. One air force that has adopted refuelling in flight for its CSAR helicopters is the Ejército del Aire (Spanish Air Force) whose KC-130 Hercules tankers now support such missions. The Eurocopter Cougar Mk.2 CSARs of the Ejército del Aire are fitted with a telescopic refuelling probe.

Since the mid-1960s and the Vietnam War, recovery of downed aircrew and infiltration/exfiltration of special forces has become an increasingly important role, with in-flight refuelling playing a major part. As well as special forces support, the Lockheed MC-130H Combat Talon II provided refuelling support to the Sikorsky MH-53J Pave Low III helicopters operating from RAF Mildenhall. (Author)

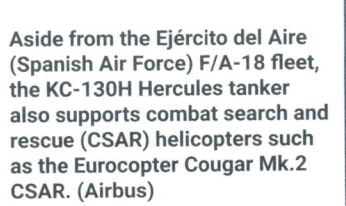

Aside from the Ejército del Aire (Spanish Air Force) F/A-18 fleet, the KC-130H Hercules tanker also supports combat search and rescue (CSAR) helicopters such as the Eurocopter Cougar Mk.2 CSAR. (Airbus)

Interestingly, prior to their transfer to the Fleet Air Arm (FAA), a few of the RAF's Merlin HC3s were fitted with a winch and a non-retractable refuelling probe in a configuration similar to that of the HH-101A operated by the Aeronautica Militare (Italian Air Force). Although the CSAR role was mooted for the RAF Merlin in the late 1990s, the type was not procured as such.

Not all in-flight refuelling involves a flying tanker. Naval helicopters, such as the Westland Sea King HAS5 could refuel while hovering alongside a ship underway. The initial step in the process is to 'earth' the helicopter to prevent the static discharges – potential ignition sources – during the refuelling process. This capability enables ships that lack a helideck, or one not rated for a helicopter class such as the Sea King, to support helicopter operations, particularly those engaged on anti-submarine tasks.

The looped-hose refuelling system survived into the 1960s in helicopter operations and enabled helicopters that lacked a refuelling probe, such as the FAA's Westland Wessex HU5, to be refuelled. The 'tanker' machine trailed a hose, and as with the original looped-hose method, the receiver deployed a grapple and caught the hose, which was then hauled into the helicopter cabin. Once the hose has been connected to the receiver's fuel system, the tanker commenced pumping fuel. As had been the case with fixed-wing aircraft, probe-and-drogue was the preferred solution for

In the late 1990s, the RAF became interested in CSAR and this AW101 Merlin HC3 was fitted with an in-flight refuelling probe and winch. The Merlin was the first RAF helicopter equipped with a refuelling probe, but requirement was not pursued, and the probes were removed. (Author)

Naval helicopters, such as the Westland Sea King HAS5, can refuel while hovering alongside a ship under way, which provides greater flexibility in anti-submarine or search-and-rescue operations. The helicopter can take on fuel from ships that either lack a helideck or are not cleared to take a machine of the Sea King's class. The helicopter crew lowers a line to the ship and the hose is then hauled into the helicopter cabin and connected to the fuel system. (Blue Envoy Collection)

in-flight refuelling and was soon adopted for helicopters. At the time of the trials, the probes were long and heavy, and structural modification would have been required for them to have been carried, which was probably not feasible for a machine the size of a Wessex.

The ability to refuel helicopters provides the US Marine Corps with a mobility and force projection in littoral warfare that is unsurpassed in any armed force. The Marine Corps can conduct 'vertical envelopment' operations by delivering marines and their support equipment from beyond the horizon to inland landing zones, thus avoiding a potentially costly beach assault.

Long out of favour for refuelling fixed-wing aircraft, the looped hose method survived into the 1960s with the Royal Navy's helicopters such as the Westland Wessex HU5. The Wessex in front has deployed the hose, which has been captured and hauled into the Wessex behind. The stabilising drogue for the end of the hose can be seen just aft of the door of the rear Wessex. Probe-and-drogue proved much simpler during operations. (Blue Envoy Collection)

The ability to refuel helicopters provides the US Marine Corps with a mobility and force projection that is unsurpassed in any armed force. The size and power of the Sikorsky CH-53E Super Stallion is evident as a pair refuels from a KC-130H Hercules while carrying a 28,000lb (12,800kg) LAV-25 armoured vehicle. The USMC can conduct 'vertical envelopment' operations by delivering marines and their support equipment from beyond the horizon to inland landing zones, thus avoiding a potentially costly beach assault. (Blue Envoy Collection)

A US Navy MH-53 Sea Dragon awaits its turn on the drogue while a Sikorsky CH-53 Super Stallion refuels from a US Marine Corps KC-130F Hercules. The drogues fitted to KC-130s for refuelling helicopters have a larger diameter than those for fast jets. Also of note is the fully extended refuelling probe. (Terry Panopalis Collection)

Helicopter refuelling was not just US Navy and Marine Corps business, as shown by a Lockheed KC-130H refuelling a Sikorsky HH-66D Night Hawk, prototype of the HH-60G Pave Hawk. All the USAF's CSAR helicopters (and special forces support helicopters) have telescopic refuelling probes. (Blue Envoy Collection)

Rotary Refuelling – Helicopters

Helicopter refuelling was not just US Navy and Marine Corps business, as the USAF had operated Sikorsky HH-3E Jolly Green Giants in the CSAR in Vietnam and the range and endurance required for rescue missions made in-flight refuelling a must. The Jolly Green Giant was superseded by the larger, more powerful HH-53 Super Jolly, which was in turn replaced by the Sikorsky HH-60G Night Hawk. All the USAF's CSAR helicopters (and special forces support helicopters) are fitted with telescopic refuelling probes.

Intended as a Hercules replacement, the A400M Atlas was also designed for the refuelling role, and its wide performance envelope enables it to receive from jet-powered tankers such as the A330 MRTT and act as a tanker for fast jets and slower aircraft such as helicopters.

Refuelling pods enable practically any aircraft that has hard points plumbed for drop tanks to conduct refuelling missions. The Airbus A400M Atlas has the speed and altitude performance range that enables it to refuel fast jets and helicopters. Airbus conducted tests with its A400M development aircraft EC-404 fitted with a 400 US gal/min (1,514l/min) Cobham 908E pod under each wing, refuelling a pair of Spanish Ejército del Aire F/A-18 Hornets. The A400M can also be fitted with the Cobham's 600 US gal/min (2,271l/min) 808E FRU in the rear of the cargo bay. While fixed-wing refuelling trials went well, work with rotary wing types was not initially successful.

Extensive trials showed that the A400M's wake turbulence affected helicopters in the refuelling position, but the problem was solved by increasing the length of the hose. Much of the development flying was carried out with Atlas EC-404 and Airbus H225 Caracal demonstrator F-ZWCS equipped with a refuelling probe for the CSAR role. (Airbus)

Chapter 9
Trials and Tankers

Much of the service acceptance trials flying for the RAF is done by the A&AEE at Boscombe Down in Wiltshire. One type earmarked for the strategic support role was the Shorts Belfast C1 and the ten Belfasts were fitted with in-flight refuelling probes. The Belfast prototype, XR363, undertook refuelling trials at the A&AEE making contacts with an HP Victor K1A. (Blue Envoy Collection)

Any aircraft being developed for military service requires rigorous pre-service trials and, if relevant, these include in-flight refuelling. These are a key process in the development programme of any combat aircraft, particularly for strategic bombers in the early years of the Cold War. Once fighters transitioned from 'scramble' interceptors to 'Barrier CAP' (combat air patrol), tankers became important to air defence and thus the fighters acquired refuelling probes, and these required testing. Ultimately, just about any aircraft aside from trainers became capable of in-flight refuelling, and all of these underwent pre-service trials.

Research and Development

Much of the service acceptance trials flying for the RAF was, until 1992, conducted by the A&AEE at Boscombe Down in Wiltshire. Since 1992, the acceptance trials have been conducted under the auspices of various agencies, most recently the Defence Science and Technology Laboratory, renamed Aircraft and Armament Evaluation Establishment.

Despite the Air Staff's initial enthusiasm for fitting them with the kit, English Electric Canberras were not used as tankers or receivers by the RAF, but FRL used the type for trials until 1971. The FRL Canberras were the only examples of the type fitted with refuelling probes and were used to train pilots

Flight Refuelling Ltd installed a Mk.16 HDU in the bomb bay of Canberra B2 WH734 to aid development of FRL equipment for aircraft such as the Gloster Javelin FAW9. Javelin XH780 is being refuelled by Canberra WH734 and interestingly the Javelin is fitted with a shorter, 'dog-legged' probe, not unlike that fitted to the McDonnell Douglas F-4 Phantom II. Trials with this style of probe showed that it was too close to the cockpit canopy and could impact on the canopy. (Jet Age Museum via Tim Kershaw)

in refuelling procedures, especially those involved in the Valiant tanker programme. In 1956, Canberra B2 WH734 was fitted with an FRL Mk.16 HDU in the bomb bay and became involved in refuelling trials for the Gloster Javelin FAW9 interceptor.

Gloster Javelin FAW9 XH965 was operated by the Ministry of Supply and used for trials of the 'lance' refuelling probe fitted to the later Javelin FAW9F/R. This sturdy item was fitted along the starboard side of the forward fuselage just below the canopy and extended forward to well beyond the radome. Javelin XH965 undertook trials of the installation at the A&AEE with Vickers Valiant B(PR)K1 WX376 as the tanker. The Javelin FAW9F/R served with Fighter Command until 1968 and was the last in the series, upgraded with the refuelling probe, drop tanks and the AI.17 radar.

RAF transports such as the Short Belfast C1 underwent A&AEE refuelling trials, while the Armstrong Whitworth Argosy C1 was tested as a tanker and receiver. Argosy XN814 was fitted out as a tanker with overload fuel tanks in the cargo compartment and an FRL Mk.20D refuelling pod on a pylon attached to the port side of the rear fuselage. The pylon was fixed to hard points that had originally been designed to carry bombs for the 'Internal Security' role, something just about every British aircraft designed in the 1950s that wasn't a fighter or bomber had to make provision for. The receiver Argosy, XN816, was fitted with a probe above the cockpit, and no major problems were reported by receiver or tanker, which refuelled a number of different types during the trials.

In-flight refuelling from Handley Page Victor K2s would be critical to the operation of the UK's new air defence fighter, the Panavia Tornado ADV. Flight refuelling trials established that the built-in retractable refuelling probe on the ADV worked as designed and ensured the Tornados could maintain barrier CAPs in the GIUK Gap. These patrols were to protect NATO convoys in the northeast Atlantic from the Soviet Naval Aviation's Tupolev Tu-142 'Bear' and Tu-22M 'Backfire' forces ranged against them. Refuelling trials involved Victor XL151 from 57 Squadron and BAe Warton's Tornado F2 prototype, ZA254.

Tankers were, and still are, crucial to the air defence of the UK and the Greenland/Iceland/UK (GIUK) Gap. The Panavia Tornado ADV was being developed in the early 1980s and, unlike the IDS versions, it was fitted with a retractable flight refuelling probe. This required testing, with BAe Warton's Tornado F2 prototype, ZA254, conducting a series of trials with Victor XL151 from 57 Sqn at Marham, demonstrating that the installation worked. (Blue Envoy Collection)

Development flying and the proving of new technologies include investigation of the entire flight envelope, especially if new control systems are involved. BAC's Active Control Technology fly-by-wire Jaguar, XX765, undertook 96 test flights, including sorties, possibly as the photoship, with Panavia Tornado ADV prototype ZA254 and a Victor tanker from 55 Sqn. (Blue Envoy Collection)

Chapter 10

Buddies

The US Navy was an early adopter of probe-and-drogue refuelling systems for its aircraft and continues to operate the system to this day. The origins of buddy-buddy refuelling between fighter/strike aircraft lay in the US Navy whose carriers could not accommodate large aircraft. The solution was to fit the refuelling kit in a drop tank that could be carried on a pylon by a strike aircraft or fighter, and this has become standard procedure for carrier aircraft. While this could work for operations around a US Navy Carrier Air Wing, deploying carrier aircraft to a war zone across an ocean required a different approach.

In what could be construed as pushing the boat out, Convair fitted four refuelling pods to a Convair R3Y Tradewind flying boat transport to produce what is possibly the first military tanker/transport. In September 1956, a Tradewind simultaneously refuelled four Grumman F9F Cougar fighters at once. The Tradewind was powered by four Allison T40 turboprop engines driving six-blade contraprops and one example, helped by the jetstream, set a transcontinental speed record in 1954 by crossing the USA with a speed of 403mph (649km/h). This record for a seaplane still stands.

The US Navy is the largest user of the buddy pack. This enables just about any carrier aircraft to become a tanker. A Lockheed S-3B Viking from VS-22 has streamed the drogue from its Sargent Fletcher pod to refuel a Grumman F-14 Tomcat from VF-32 during *Desert Storm* (DoD via Terry Panopalis Collection)

In what could be construed as pushing the boat out, Convair fitted four refuelling pods to a Convair R3Y Tradewind flying boat transport. In September 1956, a Tradewind simultaneously refuelled four Grumman F9F Cougar fighters. The Tradewind was powered by four Allison T40 turboprop engines driving six-blade contraprops and one example, helped by the jetstream, set a transcontinental speed record in 1954 by crossing the USA with a speed of 403mph (649km/h). This record for a seaplane still stands. (Blue Envoy Collection)

While adding buddy pods to flying boats enabled the US Navy to move carrier aircraft across the vast Pacific, the carrier force's operational flexibility would be increased by having its own dedicated tanker force. For this the US Navy turned to former attack aircraft such as the North American AJ-2 Savage and Douglas KA-3B Skywarrior that took over the refuelling task once they relinquished the nuclear strike role.

North American's AJ Savage was a heavy attack carrier aircraft designed to deliver the large nuclear weapons of the 1940s but later converted to the tanker role. Being powered by two Pratt & Whitney R-2800 Double Wasp piston engines and an Allison J33 turbojet, the Savage had the performance to refuel fighter aircraft such as the Vought F7U Cutlass and F8U Crusader. Although short lived in the role, the Savage was notable for refuelling Major John Glenn's Vought F8U-1P Crusader during Project Bullet, his record-breaking transcontinental flight in July 1957.

Left: Converted from the heavy attack role when the Douglas A3D entered service, the North American AJ Savage swapped nuclear weapons for a refuelling pack and carried more fuel than the contemporary Douglas AD-6 Skyraider tanker. It could refuel high-performance aircraft such as the Vought F7U Cutlass although some may argue about whether the Cutlass was high performance! (Blue Envoy Collection)

Below: The Savage did have one claim to fame during its relatively short career – Project Bullet. Savages refuelled Major John Glenn's Vought F8U-1P Crusader during his record-breaking flight. (Terry Panopalis Collection)

The US Navy's strategic bomber from 1956, until the Polaris system entered service in the early 1960s, was the Douglas A3D Skywarrior, which would become the hardest-working aircraft in the fleet. In addition to performing conventional bombing in Vietnam, the 'Whale' dropped mines, conducted electronic and photo reconnaissance, ELINT and, as the KA-3B and EKA-3B special missions aircraft, acted as a tanker for the carrier air wings. The Skywarrior was the longest serving US naval aircraft in history, finally being retired in late 1991, with its other claim to fame being that it was the heaviest naval aircraft to operate operationally from aircraft carriers.

The replacement for the A-3 Skywarrior in the bomber was the supersonic North American A-5 Vigilante, another contender for the heaviest type to operate from carriers. With the Navy's deterrent transferred to the Polaris boats, the Vigilante took on the reconnaissance role as the RA-5C and, of course, like just about every US Navy type, refuelling. The Vigilante featured a unique linear weapons

Right: Tankers ahoy! All three of these naval types are tankers, although strictly speaking only the KA-3B is a tanker; the Douglas A-4 and Supermarine Scimitar F1 are sporting buddy packs, an FRL Mk.20 on the Scimitar F1 (from 803 NAS) and a Douglas D-704 on the Skyhawk. (Blue Envoy Collection)

Below: The Skywarrior's replacement, the North American A-5A Vigilante, also took on the tanker role with tanks and HDU in the linear bomb bay. This three-ship 'daisy chain' comprises 147854, 148924 and 147853 all from VAH-7, USS *Enterprise* in 1963. (Terry Panopalis Collection)

bay, a tunnel that lay between the two J79 turbojets and could hold a nuclear weapon and up to three 295 US gal (1,117l) fuel tanks arranged along the length of the bay. With the nuclear task dropped and reconnaissance its main role, the rearmost space formerly taken up by the weapon was filled with a purpose-designed buddy refuelling unit. The Vigilante proved too expensive to operate as a tanker, and the KA-3B Skywarrior and KA-6D Intruder proved more economic in the role.

The Skywarrior was nearing retirement and having been successfully used as a buddy refueller by the US Navy, Lockheed proposed a dedicated tanker variant of the Viking to replace the 'Whale'. This involved taking the prototype YS-3 and replacing the sonobuoy dispenser package on the port side of the rear fuselage with an HDU to produce the KS-3A. After trials of the installation and refuelling of the gamut of US Navy aircraft such as the LTV A-7 Corsair, the Navy decided that the flexibility of the buddy pod provided a better solution as it retained the S-3A Viking's full anti-submarine warfare capability.

Above: Sleek and fast (it could outrun the F-4 Phantom with the same engines) the Vigilante makes a rather stunning tanker. This A-5A, 148926, from VAH-7 on USS *Enterprise* is refuelling a pair of F-8U Crusaders, also from USS *Enterprise*. In reality, the Vigilante was too expensive to operate as a tanker and better suited to reconnaissance as the RA-5C. (Terry Panopalis Collection)

Left: Lockheed tried to interest the US Navy in a tanker version of the S-3A Viking anti-submarine type. The port sonobuoy dispenser was replaced with an HDU to produce the KS-3A. The Navy preferred the flexibility of buddy pods on their aircraft, including the S-3A. (Blue Envoy Collection)

Buddies

The eventual replacement for the KA-3B Skywarrior tanker was the Grumman KA-6D Intruder, another modified strike aircraft carrying an HDU in the rear fuselage and up to five drop tanks. A total of 78 A-6As and 12 A-6Es were converted, and each Intruder unit included a couple of KA-6Ds. As the A-6 Intruders were retired in the 1990s, the S-3 Viking with buddy pods took over tanker duties pending delivery of the Boeing F/A-18 Hornet. The F/A-18 became the primary fighter and attack aircraft in US Navy service, and, to replace the KA-6D Intruder tankers, the Hornet was fitted for buddy-buddy refuelling. Like the Intruder, the Hornet could accompany the strike package on operations. Unfortunately, using Hornets as tankers took up a high proportion of the Carrier Air Wing's strike aircraft for non-strike duties.

Right: The ultimate replacement for the Skywarrior was the Grumman KA-6D Intruder, converted from A-6A and A-6E by removing the bombing system and installing refuelling equipment. This KA-6D is refuelling a Grumman F-14 Tomcat from VF-142, operating from USS *Eisenhower*. (DoD via Terry Panopalis Collection)

Below: With the A-5A dismissed from tanker duties due to expense, the upgraded RA-5C Vigilante, such as 156640 (AC602) from RVAH-12, became a reconnaissance platform. Its missions required refuelling by KA-6D Intruders such as 152934 (AC522) VA-75. This pair, both based on USS *Saratoga*, were photographed in 1987. (Terry Panopalis Collection)

An F/A-18F Super Hornet tops up a pair of F/A-18Cs in a refuelling demonstration. As the A-6 Intruder and A-7 Corsair were replaced with the McDonnell Douglas F/A-18 Hornet, a tanker to accompany strike packages was required. This led to F/A-18s being fitted with Sargent Fletcher buddy pods and four fuel tanks to act as tankers on operations. (Terry Panopalis Collection)

Boeing developed the MQ-25 Stingray UAS to act as a tanker for the fleet and free up F/A-18 Hornets for combat operations. The technicians give a good idea of the size of the Stingray and its Cobham 31-300 buddy pod. The pod is a Sargent Fletcher design, Cobham Plc having bought the company in 1994. (Cobham)

After almost 60 years in service, the Grumman E-2 Hawkeye gets a probe! Despite constant upgrades to its radar and systems, the Hawkeye only received a refuelling capability with the latest E-2D variant. (Northrop Grumman)

To free up more strike aircraft for operations, the US Navy ordered the Boeing MQ-25 Stingray refuelling drone. The US Navy, in 2006, began to investigate the use of UAVs as carrier-borne refuelling platforms in a programme that led to the Boeing MQ-25 Stingray. The Stingray, fitted with a Cobham 31-300 buddy pod, would free up Hornets and other types such as the Bell/Boeing CV-22 Osprey for offensive operations.

One US carrier type that stood out as lacking an in-flight refuelling capability for the first six decades of its career was the Grumman E-2 Hawkeye. The Hawkeye fleet has been constantly updated throughout its service with the main version being the E-2C. The revamped E-2D features a new AN/APY-9 radar and systems, plus upgraded Allison T56 engines with eight-bladed propellers. After 60 years, the Hawkeye now boasts an in-flight refuelling probe, a feature pioneered by the Israeli Air Force, for its E-2C Daya (Kite) fleet. The new probe allows Hawkeyes to refuel from US Navy KC-130s, strike aircraft such as the F/A-18 fitted with buddy packs, or the forthcoming Boeing MQ-25 Stingray UAV.

Hands Across the Sea

With many air forces using American-built naval aircraft such as the RAAF and RCAF with their Hornet fleets, one benefit of a common refuelling system amongst naval aircraft around the world is the ability to support Allied aircraft during joint operations. The US Navy and Royal Navy air wings maintained a close relationship throughout the Cold War and demonstrated this interoperability in numerous exercises. One notable occasion over the Mediterranean Sea in 1962 saw a 'daisy chain' of two US Navy and two Royal Navy aircraft.

FRL tried to interest the RAF in buddy-buddy systems, but it was the FAA that took up the buddy pack for its Sea Vixen, Scimitar and Buccaneer fleets. With the RAF ambivalent towards buddy-buddy refuelling and viewing in-flight refuelling as only suitable for large bombers and transport aircraft, the FAA adopted

Hands across the ocean. The US Navy and Royal Navy demonstrate interoperability over the Mediterranean Sea in 1962. The US aircraft from USS *Forrestal* include a McDonnell F4H-1 Phantom II from VF-74, Vought F8U-2 Crusader VF-103, Vought F8U-1P reconnaissance aircraft from VFP-62, Douglas A4D-2N Skyhawk from VA-83 and a Douglas A3D-2 Skywarrior VAH-11, with the latter two trailing hoses from their buddy packs. The Fleet Air Arm aircraft are a Supermarine Scimitar F1, XD244, from 803 Naval Air Squadron and a de Havilland Sea Vixen FAW1 from 892 NAS, both from HMS *Hermes* are also carrying buddy packs. (US Navy National Museum of Naval Aviation/DoD via Terry Panopalis)

While the RAF showed little interest in buddy pods, the Fleet Air Arm, who like the US Navy didn't need to transfer large quantities of fuel, were enthusiastic users. Scimitars and Sea Vixens, such as FAW1 XJ448, could carry a FRL Mk.20 pod. (Blue Envoy Collection)

Once the Sea Vixen had retired, the Buccaneer took on the tanker role with the same buddy pods. Operating from HMS *Ark Royal*, Blackburn Buccaneer S2B XV361 refuels Phantom FG1 XV587 (HMS *Ark Royal* photo via Terry Panopalis)

the technique with enthusiasm. FRL Mk.20A buddy pods were carried by Supermarine Scimitars and de Havilland Sea Vixens and enabled naval aircraft such as the Buccaneer to take off with a full weapons load, but light on fuel, and be topped up by a Scimitar or Sea Vixen before heading for the target.

Although the RAF had little or no interest in buddy packs per se, BAC did design a removable refuelling pack for TSR.2. This was to be carried in the weapons bay and allow TSR.2s to support each other on operations. FRL designed the Mk.26 refuelling package, which employed an HDU with a retractable boom to provide more vertical separation for the receiver aircraft. The self-contained unit could be quickly fitted in the TSR.2's weapons bay and a test article was built to check the fit on the mock-up.

Buddy refuelling was proposed for the TSR.2, and FRL designed the Mk.26 refuelling package that fitted into the weapons bay. The pack was fitted with a swing arm/boom to hold the hose away from the aircraft and increase separation between tanker and receiver. (North West Heritage Group via Joe Cherrie)

Allies and Inter-Service

While the Cold War had seen the US Navy and USAF operating in their respective areas of responsibility, exemplified by the 'Route Packages' of the Vietnam War, the wars of the last decade of the 20th century and first two decades of the 21st century saw US Navy, Marine Corps and Air Force aircraft operating as a cohesive unit alongside coalition forces. These wars, especially over Afghanistan, required continuous refuelling cover for air support aircraft operating with coalition ground forces. The diverse character of the American air forces alone meant that the on-task tankers had to cater for probe- and boom-equipped aircraft.

USAF KC-135 Stratotankers fitted with BDA could refuel probe-equipped aircraft such as US Navy McDonnell Douglas F/A-18 Hornets or RAF Tornados. The BDA uses a rigid drogue rather than the flexible basket, and it has been suggested that the shorter hose on the BDA results in easier contacts due to a much reduced manoeuvre envelope. The main problem with the KC-135/BDA is that it becomes a single-point, low flow-rate tanker. This led to many of the USAF's KC-135s being equipped with the Multi-Point Refuelling System (MPRS) comprising a Cobham Mk.32B pod under each wing. This installation enabled probe-equipped aircraft to refuel in pairs while retaining the boom for USAF aircraft such as the Fairchild A-10A Thunderbolt II close support aircraft.

Left: The incompatibility of boom and probe/drogue refuelling systems was solved by fitting boom-equipped aircraft with HDUs, as with the KC-10, or as shown here refuelling a pair of RAF Tornado GR4s, the Multi-Point Refuelling System (MPRS) on the KC-135. (DoD/USAF)

Below: Operation *Telic/Iraqi Freedom* saw US and UK aircraft operating in concert to protect and support ground troops. Tankers, such as this KC-10 fitted with wing air refuelling pods, refuelled the various coalition air assets such as this USAF B-1B Lancer and a pair of RAF Tornado F3s. The B-1B is on the Extender's boom, while the Tornados will use either the centreline HDU or the wing tip refuelling pods. (Terry Panopalis Collection)

Buddies

RAF aircraft operating over Iraq during Operation *Telic* were frequent users of the USAF's tanker force, especially KC-135s fitted with the MPRS. The RAF reciprocated with TriStars and VC10s refuelling US probe-equipped types such as US Navy McDonnell Douglas F/A-18C Hornets. Throughout the wars since 2001, coalition air forces have successfully operated as a unified force, a force multiplied by co-ordination of refuelling whereby the two different systems – flying boom and probe-and-drogue – have been combined on the tankers themselves to allow an aircraft, fitted with whichever system, to refuel.

Right: The West's carrier forces have shared resources for decades, be it cross decking between ships or, as shown here, refuelling. A pair of Aéronautique Navale Dassault Super Etendards from *Clemenceau* refuelling from a Grumman KA-6D of VA-34 on USS *George Washington*. (US Navy via Terry Panopalis)

Below: The Fleet Air Arm and US Navy have worked closely since the Second World War, particularly in the air. This Douglas KA-3B from VAH-2 refuels Blackburn Buccaneer XT279 from 801 NAS based on HMS *Victorious*. (FAA via Terry Panopalis Collection)

Chapter 11
Dozapravka vs Polete

As was the case with the SAC, the Soviet Dal'naya Aviatsiya Vozdushnikh Syl (Long-Range Aviation of Air Forces) required aircraft to carry nuclear weapons deep into 'enemy' territory. Similarly, two refuelling systems evolved in the Soviet Union: probe-and-drogue (as per the Western system) and wing tip-to-wing tip. The latter, a variation on the looped-hose method, was the forte of the Tupolev design bureau and used on the Tu-16 'Badger', with the tanker designated Tu-16Z. This specialist variant carried a hose drum in the fuselage. The hose was fed to a fairing at the starboard wing tip from which the equipment was trailed, stabilised by a small drogue parachute.

The Tupolev refuelling technique was reminiscent of ships undergoing replenishment at sea and involved a 'shot line', complete with drogue chute, attached to the coupling at the end of the hose. The HDU in the bomb bay fed the hose out along the starboard wing to the hose guide on the wing tip. The drogue chute stabilised the hose as it was streamed behind the tanker on the 40m (130ft) shot line, similar to a cable used to haul hoses between ships underway. The receiver drew up alongside the end of the hose and, guided by the tail gunner, the pilot positioned the port wing tip over the hose. Under the receiver's wing tip, a device with a latch captured the receiver's end of the hose and coupled it to the refuelling receptacle. The shot line was hauled in by the tanker, and the other end of the hose coupled to the fuel feed on the tanker. The Tupolev refuelling system was complex and even dangerous, but once the ends of the hose were connected, the spectacle took on a rather graceful appearance.

The Tupolev Tu-16Z 'Badger' used the wing tip-to-wing tip system that required some intricate manoeuvres. The penultimate stage of this procedure shown here has the receiver, Tu-16R (Black 21), with the hose captured and coupled while the Tu-16Z tanker (Black 30), reels in the shot line. Once connected, fuel can be transferred. (Via Yefim Gordon)

Tupolev's Tu-16Z tanker showing the wing tip fairing that housed the drogue and hose. The Tupolev system was not adopted by any other air force and remained unique to the Tu-16Z as wings on other types such as the Tu-95 'Bear' flexed too much in flight. The method was dispensed with and the Tu-16Z converted to Tu-16N with a drogue-equipped refuelling pod under each wing. (Via Yefim Gordon)

The system was installed on two operational types, the Tu-4 'Bull' (a reverse-engineered Boeing B-29 Superfortress) and the Tu-16 'Badger'. The procedure required very skilful flying on the receiver's part as the process took place approximately 52ft (15.8m) to port and 59ft (18m) aft of the receiver's cockpit. The tanker was required to conduct a number of separate stages to prepare for a fuel transfer. The Tu-16Z had, by 1963, been replaced by the Tu-16N, which featured a probe-and-drogue system with an HDU in the bomb bay and operated by Soviet Naval Aviation (Aviatsiya voyenno-morskogo flota) in support of maritime operations by Tupolev Tu-22 'Blinder' and Tu-22M 'Backfire' missile carriers. One of the reasons (aside from its complexity) the Tupolev wing tip system failed to prosper was wing flex, particularly on larger aircraft like the Tu-95 'Bear' due to its high aspect ratio wings flexing too much at the tip.

The Soviets, like the British, used converted bombers for in-flight refuelling, and to carry out probe-and-drogue refuelling of large aircraft, the Myasishchev M-4 'Bison' was fitted with an HDU in the bomb bay. Gauging by the diameter and length of the hose, the HDU must have been a sizeable piece of kit and the 'Bison' remained a single-point tanker for its entire career. The 'Bison A' bomber could only just reach the United States and lacked the range to carry weapons to targets deep inside the USA, and so most were converted to tankers. The 'Bison B' tanker fleet supported Soviet types such as the Tupolev Tu-95 'Bear' and Tu-126 'Moss' AEW aircraft, both of which were fitted with refuelling probes. The 'Bison' fleet supported Soviet and Russian bomber and reconnaissance operations until 1994, by which time it had been replaced by the three-point Ilyushin Il-78 'Midas'.

The standard Ilyushin Il-76 'Candid' transport had been adapted as a tanker but was limited in its 'disposable' fuel load. In response, Ilyushin developed the Il-78 'Midas' tanker/transport that carried two removable fuel tanks in the freight hold and offered three times the available fuel load of the

Left: The probe extending aft of the starboard wing tip of the Tupolev Tu-16Z holds the stabilising drogue parachute for the shot line used for the initial contact between the tanker and receiver. (Via Yefim Gordon)

Below: Myasishchev M4 'Bison-A' strategic bombers were converted into tankers to refuel the Soviet Long-Range Aviation's fleet of strategic bombers. These 'Bison-B' tankers carried a HDU in the bomb bay and refuelled not only Tupolev Tu-95 'Bear' bomber and reconnaissance aircraft but also the Tupolev Tu-126 'Moss' AEW aircraft operated by the Soviet Air Defence Forces. (Via Yefim Gordon)

The size of the M-4 'Bison's bomb bay is apparent from the length of hose trailed from the 'Bison B' tanker. Estimates from this photo produce a length of approximately 30m (100ft) of large diameter hose, which is a considerable amount of hose to spool onto an HDU! The large hose diameter is required to maximise the fuel transfer rate but limited in length by the HDU spool capacity. This was the USAF's rationale for adopting the flying boom for its bomber aircraft. (Via Yefim Gordon)

'Candid' tanker. The Il-78 was fitted with three UPAZ-1A refuelling pods, one under each outer wing and a third mounted on a stub wing on the port side of the rear fuselage. Interestingly, with shades of the Hercules C1K, the Iraqi Air Force independently developed a tanker version of the Il-76MD 'Candid' by fitting a buddy pod (procured for the Iraqi AF's Mirage F1 fleet) on the cargo ramp.

China's People's Liberation Army – Air force (PLA-AF) has been increasing its refuelling capability in line with the modernisation of its air forces. Tanker versions of the Xi'an H-6 (a licence-built Tupolev Tu-16 'Badger') fitted with underwing refuelling pods are operated by the PLA-AF and Naval Air Force (PLA-NAF) as the HY-6U and HY-6D respectively. Given the limited fuel capacity of the HY-6 series, the PLA-AF acquired three Ilyushin Il-78 'Midas' and embarked on a tanker variant of the Xi'an Y-20 transport, apparently using a three-point refuelling configuration similar to the Ilyushin Il-78 'Midas'.

The UPAZ-1M pod is interesting in that rather than using an external propeller to drive the generator that powered the pod's winch and pump, it uses an internal ram-air turbine. The pod's nose cone retracts to allow mass flow into the ram-air turbine within the pod, a configuration that provides much lower drag than the propeller driven systems of the West. The UPAZ-M pod can also be carried as a buddy pod by strike aircraft such as the Sukhoi Su-24M 'Fencer-D' or its replacement, the Su-34 'Fullback'.

In addition to supporting Long-Range Aviation, the Ilyushin Il-78M 'Midas' supported Soviet and Russian deep strike aircraft such as the Sukhoi Su-24M 'Fencer-D'. The modernised Su-24M first flew in 1979, becoming the first variant to incorporate a retractable in-flight refuelling probe, and its inclusion gave the 'Fencer-D' a much-improved deep strike capability. When combined with new precision-guided munitions, the 'Fencer' became a formidable strike aircraft that in the 1980s was viewed by NATO as a serious threat to airfields and installations in Western Europe.

The Il-78 'Midas' can also refuel the heavier end of the spectrum including the Tupolev Tu-95 'Bear' and other larger types in the inventory of the Russian air forces. (Via Yefim Gordon)

The UPAZ-1M Sakhalin refuelling pod shown on an Ilyushin Il-78M 'Midas' wing pylon. The UPAZ-1M is interesting in that rather than using an external propeller to drive the generator that powered the hose-drum's winch and the pump, it uses a ram-air turbine within the body. The pod's nose cone retracts to allow mass flow into the ram-air turbine within the pod. The UPAZ-M pod can also be carried as a buddy pod by strike aircraft such as the Sukhoi Su-24M 'Fencer-D' or its replacement, the Su-34 'Fullback'.

The Ilyushin Il-78 'Midas' is a three-point tanker but uses a UPAZ pod on the fuselage station rather than an internal HDU. This 'Midas' is in contact with a pair of Sukhoi Su-27 'Flanker' fighters and a Su-34 'Fullback' strike aircraft. (Via Yefim Gordon)

A more capable tanker than its predecessors, the Ilyushin Il-78 'Midas' could provide support to a wider range of aircraft. One type, the Sukhoi Su-24M 'Fencer-D', benefitted from the addition of a retractable refuelling probe and 'Midas' support. Air-to-air refuelling would have allowed the 'Fencer' to penetrate even deeper into NATO territory. (Blue Envoy Collection via Yefim Gordon)

Chapter 12

Les Revitailleurs – Sous-Marine

For an air force with no aircraft (aside from its own tankers) fitted for flying boom refuelling, the choice of the Boeing KC-135 for l'Armée de l'Air (AdlA) might appear odd, but they came fitted with the BDA to refuel the Force de Frappe's Mirage IV bombers. Of the four export customers for the Boeing KC-135, only France bought new-build KC-135s, designated C-135F and configured as tanker/transports from the start. For cost reasons, the AdlA's 12 C-135Fs were powered by the Pratt & Whitney J57 turbojet rather than the Pratt & Whitney TF33 turbofan that had been specified when purchased in 1964. From 1985, AdlA, like the USAF, re-engined its 11 surviving C-135Fs with the CFM International CFM56 turbofan replacing the Pratt & Whitney J57 turbojet to produce the C-135FR. Aside from 22,500lbf (100kN) more thrust, the CFM56's fuel efficiency enabled a 50% increase in fuel offload on long missions. The C-135FR was given a further upgrade in 2014 with new systems installed in the US to produce the C-135RG. A further three USAF-surplus KC-135Rs were procured to bring the total in the fleet to 14, and the type has been enhanced by fitting the MPRS.

The original Sous-Marine. l'Armee de l'Air received 12 KC-135Fs, all fitted with the original J57 turbojets designated C-135F. All were fitted with the flying boom with BDA as shown on 63-12736, which is about to refuel a Jaguar A. (Terry Panopalis Collection)

Like the USAF with its J57-powered KC-135s, in 1985 l'Armee de l'Air started to re-engine its 11 surviving C-135Fs with the CFM International CFM56 turbofan to produce the C-135FR. The new engines provided more thrust and more endurance, as well as making more fuel available for offload, and with an avionics upgrade, the C-135FRs gained a new lease of life as C-135RGs. These also acquired MPRS pods, as seen here refuelling a Mirage 2000 and a Mirage IV. (Via Robert S Hopkins III)

The French Air Force of the 1970s not only used its C-135Fs to support the Mirage IVA fleet of the Force de Frappe, but also tactical aircraft such at the SEPECAT Jaguar A and the Mirage F1 (behind the Mirage IVA, probe in the BDA). The C-135F was a tanker/transport, and for cost reasons the ALAT's C-135Fs were powered by the Pratt & Whitney J57 turbojet rather than the Pratt & Whitney TF33 turbofan. (Via Robert S Hopkins III)

Chapter 13

The 707 Tankers

While the KC-135 was developed as a dedicated tanker, Boeing used the basic idea to produce the 707 airliner that plied the airways for decades. In the 1970s, airlines began to trade their 707s for 747s, TriStars and DC-10s, which meant that a lot of low hours 707s were available. Bedek Aviation, a subsidiary of Israeli Aerospace Industries, offered tanker conversions of these Boeing 707s, initially for the Israeli Air Force, but also made the conversions available to other countries. The Boeing 707 can be fitted with wing pods, a Boeing flying boom system or both. Many modern air forces operate American aircraft with either boom receptacles or probes, and very few have the facilities for both. The solution is to have a centreline-mounted flying boom and drogue pods under the wings. One of the earliest examples was the Bedek Aviation conversion of the Boeing 707, which greatly increases the flexibility in operations and enables air forces with a mixed fleet of aircraft to operate efficiently.

Boom-equipped 707s of the Israeli Air Force refuelled ten McDonnell Douglas F-15 *Baz* (eight for the attack, two in reserve) for Operation *Wooden Leg*, the 1982 attack on the Palestinian Liberation Organisation's headquarters in Tunis. Bedek Aviation also converted Boeing 707s to three-point probe-

In the 1980s, many modern air forces operated American aircraft with either boom receptacles or probes, and very few have the facilities for both. The solution is to have a centreline-mounted flying boom and drogue pods under the wings. One of the earliest examples was the Bedek Aviation conversion of the Boeing 707, seen here with a General Dynamics F-16 on the boom and two Douglas A-4N Skyhawks on the drogues. (Blue Envoy Collection)

For services that only used probe-and-drogue refuelling, Bedek Aviation converted Boeing 707s to three-point tankers. The conversion comprised an FRL Mk.32 pod under each wingtip and a Mk.34 HDU in the rear fuselage. Refuelling three aircraft was demonstrated by two Douglas TA-4J Skyhawks and a Douglas A-4N of the Israeli Air Force. (Blue Envoy Collection)

Following on from their earlier work, Bedek Aviation converted four of the Royal Australian Air Force's Boeing 707 transports into three-point tankers. These proved ideal as support for the RAAF's McDonnell Douglas F/A-18 Hornet fleet on deployments and latterly on operations over Afghanistan, where they refuelled RAAF and Coalition aircraft. The 707s were operated by 33 Squadron and one example, EB-707 A20-629, is shown here refuelling a US Navy F/A-18C Hornet from VFA-131 based on USS *John F. Kennedy* in 2002. (US Navy/DoD)

and-drogue refuellers with an FRL Mk.32 pod under each wing tip and a Mk.34 HDU in the rear fuselage.

The RAAF acquired eight Boeing 707 airliners and contracted Israeli Aerospace Industries/Bedek Aviation to convert four of these into tankers. They were used to support the RAAF on operations including regular RAAF deployments to Malaysia and the Middle East. The RAAF's F/A-18 Hornet fleet were regular receivers from 33 Squadron 707s, but the Boeings also refuelled coalition aircraft over Afghanistan, especially carrier aircraft from US carriers operating in the Arabian Sea.

The RCAF also used the Boeing 707 as a tanker/transport with Beech Model 1080 ARS fitted on the wing tips of Boeing 707s, which the RCAF called the CC-137 Husky. The RCAF acquired five CC-137 Huskies but only had two pairs of refuelling pods, which were rotated around the fleet to spread the use of the capability. From 1995, the Husky was replaced with the Airbus CC-150 Polaris. The Islamic Republic of Iran Air Force (IRIAF) still operates at least one Boeing 707-3J9C equipped with the Beech 1080 ARS on each wing tip, plus a flying boom under the rear fuselage. The IRIAF also operates the sole surviving Boeing KC-747, which is similar to the KC-33 developed as a bid for the Advanced Tanker Cargo Aircraft requirement. Iran bought four 747s in the late 1970s to support its F-4 Phantom fleet, and they saw use in the 1980–88 Iran–Iraq War. It is thought that one KC-747 remains operational.

Another 707 variant in use as a tanker is the KE-3A. When Saudi Arabia ordered five Boeing E-3A Sentries to provide AEW for the Royal Saudi Air Force, they also ordered eight Boeing KE-3A tankers, which were powered by the TF33 turbofan. Like the RAF and AdlA E-3s, the Saudi Sentries and the KE-3s were powered by CFM56 turbofans and fitted with a Boeing flying boom on the centreline and a Beech 1080 ARS pod under each wing tip.

A variation on the buddy pack was the Beech Model 1080 ARS fitted on the wing tips of Boeing 707 Tanker Transports. This Royal Canadian Air Force CC-137 Husky, 13704, is using ARS to refuel a pair of Canadair CF-118s (licence-built Northrop F-5s). The two Boeing 707-3J9C Tanker Transports of the Islamic Republic of Iran Air Force were fitted with the Beech ARS and a flying boom. (Terry Panopalis Collection)

A new tactical transport appeared on the scene in 2015 in the shape of the Embraer C-390. The C-390 can be configured with a refuelling probe above the cockpit as a receiver and as a tanker with the addition of underwing Cobham 912E refuelling pods, becoming the KC-390. In late 2019, Boeing and Embraer entered a joint venture to market the C-390 under the name Millenium. The KC-390 can refuel fast jets such as the Brazilian Air Force's Northrop F-5EM, as seen here, or slower aircraft such as helicopters. (Embraer)

The New and Future Generations

The Lockheed KC-130 Hercules established the tactical transport aircraft in the tanker role back in the 1960s, and since then every new tactical transport aircraft has acquired the capability. Embraer's KC-390 is in the same weight class as the Hercules, and, as expected, can be fitted with underwing refuelling pods. The KC-390 is fitted with a refuelling probe above the port side of the cockpit. Such is the performance envelope of the turbofan-powered KC-390 that it can refuel fast jets like the Brazilian Air Force's Northrop F-5EM or slower aircraft such as helicopters.

Handball to Hands-Off

As described above, any air force that hopes to be taken seriously as a fighting force requires a tanker force, be it to keep its ground support types on station to assist ground troops, interceptors in the right place to shepherd intruders, or merely enable aircraft to deploy for exercises. Tankers have come a long way from wing walkers 'handballing' cans of petrol between biplanes to automatic, hands-off refuelling at speeds and altitudes – not to mention transfer rates – that the wing walkers could only dream of. Since the Second World War, tankers have contributed much to air force operations and made missions that were thought impossible possible. Tankers are a significant force multiplier, and as such they allow an air force to perform at a level beyond its on-paper strength.

Conclusion

From being specific to the USAF in 1947, the tanker as a force multiplier in its tanker/transport guise, has spread to air forces around the world. Those with no day-to-day need for air-to-air refuelling can now hire the capability on an ad hoc basis or, as is the case with the RAF, farm it out to commercial organisations. *'Nobody kicks ass without tanker gas'*, the motto of the KC-135 crews, has probably never been more apt in the 2020s.

Perhaps the finest example of a country using force multipliers is Singapore. The Republic of Singapore Air Force has one of the most modern fleets in the world. These RSAF KC-135s have been replaced by the A330 MRTT and are to be upgraded with the Airbus Automatic Refuelling System. (RSAF via Robert S Hopkins III)

Select Bibliography

Butler, P and Buttler, T, *Handley Page Victor – the Crescent Winged V-Bomber*, Aerofax (2009)

Butler, P and Buttler, T, *Avro Vulcan: Britain's Famous Delta Wing V-Bomber*, Aerofax (2007)

Buttler and Rupprecht, *Dragon's Wings: Chinese Fighter and Bomber Aircraft Development*, Classic Publications (2013)

Francillon, R J, *Lockheed Aircraft since 1913*, Putnam Publishing (1982)

Francillon, R J, *McDonnell Douglas Aircraft since 1920 – Volumes I and II*, Putnam Publishing (1988)

Gibson, C, *Battle Flight*, Hikoki Publications (2012)

Gibson, C, *Vickers VC10 – AEW, Pofflers and Other Unbuilt Variants*, Blue Envoy Press (2009)

Gordon, Y and Komissarov, D, *Chinese Aircraft: History of China's Aviation Industry 1951-2007*, Hikoki Publishing (2007)

Gordon, Y, *OKB Tupolev: A History of the Design Bureau and Its Aircraft*, Midland Publishing (2005)

Gunston, B, *Cambridge Aerospace Dictionary*, Cambridge University Press (2004)

Hopkins, R S, *Boeing KC-135 – More than just a Tanker*, Crecy Publishing (2016)

Jarret, P (Ed), *The Modern War Machine*, Putnam Aeronautical Books (2000)

Morgan, E, *Vickers Valiant: The First V-bomber*, Aerofax (2002)

Tanner, R M, *History of Air-to-Air Refuelling*, Pen and Sword (2006)

Journals and Magazines

Aeroplane, various issues, Key Publishing

Air Forces Monthly, various issues, Key Publishing

International Air Power Review, various issues, Aerospace Publishing

Wings of Fame, various issues, Aerospace Publishing

World Air Power Journal, various issues, Aerospace Publishing

Glossary

A&AEE	Aircraft & Armament Experimental Establishment
AARB	Advanced Aerial Refuelling Boom
AARBS	Advanced Aerial Refuelling Boom System
ADIZ	Air Defence Identification Zone
AdlA	Armée de l'Air (French Air Force)
ARS	Beech Aerial Refuelling System
ASR	Air Staff Requirement
AST	Air Staff Target
BDA	Boom-to-Drogue Adapter
CCTV	Closed Circuit Television
CSAR	Combat Search and Rescue
ECM	Electronic Countermeasures
FAA	Fleet Air Arm
FRL	Flight Refuelling Ltd
FRU	Fuselage Refuelling Unit
FSTA	Future Strategic Tanker Aircraft
GIUK	Greenland–Iceland–UK
HDU	Hose Drum Unit
IRIAF	Islamic Republic of Iran Air Force
MAC	Military Airlift Command
MPRS	Multi-Point Refuelling System
MRTT	Multi-Role Tanker Transport
PLA-AF	People's Liberation Army – Air force
QRA	Quick Reaction Alert
RAAF	Royal Australian Air Force
RAF	Royal Air Force
RCAF	Royal Canadian Air Force
RNLAF	Royal Netherlands Air Force
SAC	Strategic Air Command
Surge Fleet	Three (previously four) Voyagers used for civil charter work by AirTanker plc.
TAC	Tactical Air Command
UAV	Uninhabited Air Vehicle
USAAF	United States Army Air Force
USAF	United States Air Force
USMC	United States Marine Corps
USSR	Union of Soviet Socialist Republics
X-ray	An unidentified track that approaches or enters NATO air space